when life Roars Jesus whispers

Sh! Listen to His gentle whispers

Kathi

1 Kings 19:12

WHEN LIFE ROARS, JESUS WHISPERS

KATHI WALIGORA

BVB

BOLD VISION BOOKS
PO BOX 2011
FRIENDSWOOD, TEXAS 77549

TABLE OF CONTENTS

The next time you find yourself alone in a dark alley facing the undeniables of life, don't cover them with a blanket, or ignore them with a nervous grin. Instead, stand still, whisper His name, and listen. He is nearer than you think.

~MAX LUCADO

The Wind ~ The Earthquake ~ The Fire

I washed fifty loads of laundry that first week. Towels, sheets, bedding, clothing, anything and everything washable I had taken out of their house, which I had come to call the *pit*. The *pit* where my darling grandchildren had lived—the *pit* where my once-beautiful daughter and her husband had used meth—the *pit* I prayed my daughter and my grandchildren would never enter again.

I packed it all in garbage bags—the dirty and the clean—all to be laundered. It's important to save everything, I told myself. Amber will need her household linens. The children will need their clothing. We can't buy everything new for them. Besides, they like their clothes. They need familiarity. I'll sort and match later. Then we'll buy whatever else they need. And we did.

Looking at Elijah

Elijah, a mighty prophet of God, had seen God's miraculous power. By that power, Elijah had breathed life into the widow's dead son; had halted the rain for years by speaking in the name of the Lord God of Israel; and had called down the fire of the Lord, which had burned up the water-drenched sacrifices offered by the prophets of the false god, Baal. But evil persists. Even after these holiest of victories Elijah, when later frightened by evil, ran and hid in a cave.

Now I was frightened by evil, and I wanted to hide! I simply could not confront the turmoil suddenly cast upon me. In studying Elijah, I found lessons of truth for myself:

"Elijah was afraid and ran for his life . . . There he went into a cave and spent the night. . . . The Lord said, 'Go out and stand on the mountain in the presence of the Lord, for the Lord is about to pass by.' Then a great and powerful wind tore the mountains apart and shattered the rocks before the Lord, but the Lord was not in the wind. After the wind there was an earthquake, but the Lord was not in the earthquake.

After the earthquake came a fire, but the Lord was not in the fire. And after the fire came a gentle whisper." *Where are you now, Lord?* I wondered. *Where are you now— in the midst of my storm?*

And Jesus Whispered

Kathi, I was not in the great and powerful wind, the earthquake, or the fire, which tore your world apart and shattered you; but I was with you through it all, and I am with you now. Listen to me.

So I quieted myself and began to listen to His gentle whisper. And it first spoke of truth.

chapter one

Whispers of Truth
Facing Truth in the Darkness

I would have every Christian wish to know
all that he can know of revealed truth. Some-
body whispers that the secret things belong
not to us. You may be sure you will never
know them if they are secret; but all that is
revealed you ought to know for these things
belong to you and to your children. Take care
you know what the Holy Ghost teaches. Do
not give way to a faint-hearted ignorance, lest
you be great losers thereby.
~CHARLES HADDON SPURGEON

I would have preferred "faint-hearted ignorance" to the *bold-faced* truth. It would have been so much easier that way. I did not want to think of my daughter, Amber, using *any* drug, let alone, meth. And I certainly did not want to think of anything bad happening to her or to her husband, Jesse, or especially to the children. And so, I had prayed for years. On my knees, day and night, I had begged the Lord to keep them safe, and He had, in spite of the perilous position in which they dwelt.

I yearned for nights filled with peaceful sleep and pleasant dreams of beautiful moments, dreams of my family gathered together, everyone healthy and happy, like a Christian family *should* be or *could* be, but in reality, it wasn't so. Instead of sleeping peacefully and dreaming pleasant dreams, I usually tossed and turned. This night was no different.

The phone call came shortly after Ron and I were both sound asleep, early in the night, between a normal Tuesday and a wretched Wednesday. I jumped out of bed to answer. With Mama and Daddy in the nursing home, I was accustomed to receiving phone calls day or night. "Doctor ordered a different medicine," or "Your mother had a fall." But I could see on the caller ID that this call was different. It was Jesse's dad, Jake. I knew something was wrong—desperately wrong.

"Kathi, this is Jake. Amber and Jesse have been arrested."

Please, God, let this be a nightmare. Let me wake up now.

"Amber called around 1:00 a.m. She asked me to come over and get the kids."

Did they cry? Was there a scene? Police? Flashing lights? Guns drawn? I want to hold my grandchildren in my arms. My cheeks on their cheeks.

"CPS was there."

CPS? Child Protective Services?

"Deputies were still there when I left. They'd already taken Jesse to jail. They were ready to take Amber after I left."

My Amber in jail? My darling daughter in jail?

"I brought the kids to my house," he continued. "They're in bed now. I think they're asleep."

13

I want to go get the kids. I want to bring them here. No, they're okay with Jake. They're sleeping. I hope *they're sleeping.*

"Arrested for what, Jake?"

The sound of my own voice startled me; I was surprised I was able to speak. I was now also talking to Ron who had sat up in bed, at the same time I spoke to Jake.

I knew the answer to my question. *It must be drugs. What drugs? I hope it's only marijuana.*

"Meth."

Oh, God, no. Please, no.

My wide-awake nightmare continued. Jesse had been taken to jail first and had tested positive for drugs. Deputies had stayed at the house and questioned Amber. They searched the house and found remnants of drugs and drug paraphernalia.

Drugs?

CPS came and instructed Amber to call the nearest relative. Amber was then asked to awaken each child, say goodbye, and send them with their other grandpa, Jake. In the middle of a cold winter night, Jake had taken the children to his house, blocks away.

I don't remember any more of the conversation. I hung up the phone.

Maybe I've misunderstood. Maybe it's not as bad as it sounds.

I quickly dialed Amber's number. She answered. She cried. I spoke with the deputy. I asked questions. I had not misunderstood. They were ready to take her to jail.

Please be careful with my daughter. Lord God, please keep her safe.

I again spoke to Amber. "We will help you get through this, honey. God loves you. Daddy and I love you."

Goodbye, my precious daughter.

14

Ron and I cried. My heart sank to a depth in my soul that I hadn't known existed. We lay in our bed, which now felt like a cement slab, and we held each other for the rest of the night in shock, in silence, in dismay.

> *Night is a time of rigor, but also of mercy.*
> *There are truths which one can see only when*
> *it's dark.*
> ~ISAAC BASHEVIS SINGER[1]

FACING the DEMON

We had known they were depressed. The depression had begun years before and had sprung its ugly head up again and again until finally it had overtaken them. Now we knew why. It was the demon of the drug.

Twelve years earlier, Ron and I had started what became a thriving business in the historic downtown district in Coldwater, Michigan. We had purchased, refurbished, and redesigned a large, 1879 Victorian building to house a coffee shop, small restaurant, and beautiful retail store. We named the business North Woods Coffee Co. The business soared in a short time. The entire experience was new to us. Ron had a business background in Semi Parts and Service; I had been a teacher. We left those professions and together took on this new venture. Our youngest daughter, Amber, was our key employee. A young mother, Amber was busy with her two-year-old son; nonetheless, she helped us get our business going, and she excelled in every aspect of our business, as barista, supervisor of our restaurant, retail clerk, and most importantly, in overseeing all of our bookwork. Those first years were blessed for us. Amber was faithful and took pride in her work. She had a delightful personality. The customers loved her. We couldn't imagine running the business without her.

Two years into the business, Amber and Jesse had their second child, another sweet baby boy. Shortly thereafter, we began to notice changes in them—undesirable changes. Her declining work ethic was our first clue to the change. We initially attributed this to her added responsibilities at home, but we discovered the changes were much deeper than we knew. Amber started coming to work late. Sometimes she never came at all. She didn't answer her home phone. Since we paid Amber hourly, her paycheck diminished. Occasionally we drove to their house in Bronson to check on her and the kids. We took food. We hugged the kids and her. Amber avoided eye contact with us. I knew why. She was humiliated, and I was embarrassed for her. The house was cluttered with fast food leftovers and bags. Sinks were stained. Dirty dishes covered the stove top and counters. I never commented about it. I didn't chastise her. Sometimes I washed dishes or tidied the living room. Jesse was usually gone when we visited, especially if we called first and left a message that we were coming.

Meanwhile, Jesse was slacking in his own work ethic. He was also employed in a family business, owned by his dad and mom, Jake and Cyndi. Jesse, like Amber, started coming to work late or missed work completely. This led to family disagreements and arguments within his family. Harsh words were spoken. Jesse was fired.

Our business was still growing and struggling as any new restaurant or retail store does. Without Amber's diligence, we were overwhelmed. I had resigned my teaching position to start this business, which meant I had given up our health insurance. Now, Ron and I paid not only our own health insurance, but Amber's and her family's health insurance, as well. We were barely meeting all our expenses of the business and had little income of our own. Ron and I had invested everything we had in this new business, including all of our physical strength. We were worn out from 16-18 hour days during the first years. Waking at 4:30 a.m., we rushed to open at 7 a.m., with smiles on our faces, ready for our regular customers. We both worked ourselves ragged all day, leaving the store about 9:30 p.m. By the third year, we were a bit more organized and consequently able to leave the store by 6 p.m., delegating the closing responsibilities to our evening supervisor.

This routine continued day after day. On Sundays, our business was closed to the public, but after church we most often went to the store and worked for the rest of the day. Occasionally, our older children came to visit us at the store on Sunday afternoons. They couldn't visit us at home because we were rarely there. Kristen and Josh came often. Matt and Lynette came with two of our grandchildren. Family life was as close to normal as it could be at this time. They were understanding of our obligations to our business, and on these occasional Sunday afternoon visits, the girls often helped me set up displays or the boys helped Ron work on an icemaker or move a heavy cabinet. We cherished the short times we had together. But most Sunday afternoons, Ron and I worked all afternoon to get ready for the coming week. Our business was demanding and exhausting, taking every bit of our being. We took no rest from it, so we grew physically and emotionally drained. Oh, how we wished we didn't have the added burdens Amber and Jesse were bringing to themselves, which in turn affected us. It was difficult to *parent* at this stage of our lives.

After some time, Jesse went back to work. We encouraged Amber in her own work ethic and responsibility.

Ron was patient and forgiving with Amber, as he was with all our employees. I had high hopes for Amber. We both did. But by this time, Amber and Jesse had not paid their mortgage for several months. They were losing their home. That meant our two little grandsons were also losing their home. Ron and I went to the bank and paid their past mortgage payments. We hoped to give them a fresh start.

We were hopeful.

But the ugly head of the demon of drugs and depression raised up again and would not back off for quite some time.

FACING the FLAMES

At the end of the sixth year, we sold our business. What a relief it was to us! Ron took a position, selling semis. I began adjunct teaching at two colleges. The heavy yoke of the business was gone, but not the burden we still carried for our youngest daughter and her family. Amber and Jesse's old habits had returned. Jesse again lost his job. And during those last years of our business, Amber had again been irresponsible at work. I had once again attributed it to change—this time, her third pregnancy. A beautiful baby girl was born the month after our business sold. *Now they are on their own,* I thought. *Amber no longer works for us. She and Jesse will be forced to stand on their own two feet and be responsible parents and citizens.* But they were not.

I was ending a class at a college where I taught, when I received a call on my cell. It was Amber, and she rarely called me, so I was alarmed.

"Mom, our house is on fire. Flames are shooting through the roof."

I rushed to Bronson, about 40 miles away. On the way, I called Ron and prayed aloud. "Please. God. Keep them all safe." Ron and I arrived at their house in Bronson at the same time. The children were safe. *Thank you, God.* The fire had started in a television cord, in the upstairs playroom. Amber and Jacob, the oldest, and baby Kaylee were gone when the fire started. Benny, then five years old, woke his dad, Jesse, who was asleep on the couch. Jesse first took Benny outdoors to safety, then went upstairs to try to put the fire out. He inhaled a great deal of smoke in his futile attempt, but he, too, was now safe. I was impressed with Jesse's efforts, especially in getting Benny out of the house first. We watched Jesse and his friends board up the damaged house. Then we went to Jake and Cyndi's house a few blocks away. We discussed insurance details and thanked God all were safe. *Maybe this frightening ordeal will turn their lives around.*

Again, I was hopeful.

Dealing with the insurance company was excruciating for Amber. And for me. In the past, I had completed much paperwork to attain both Bachelor and Master degrees, had developed educational curriculum, had prepared a lengthy business plan for the store, and had filled out unending Veterans Administration, Nursing Home, and Medicaid forms for both of my parents, but I had never encountered obstacles and dead ends like Amber faced with their insurance company. It was like a bad dream when you try to get somewhere but you can't move. I tried to offer advice and direction, but it was difficult for even me to know how to get past all the obstacles thrown in front of them. Amber and Jesse, in their states of depression, did not handle it well. It was eighteen long months before they would once again live in their home. Those months were the worst of their despair thus far.

Within a week after the fire, Amber and Jesse had settled into a rental home in the country. It was a pleasant setting. The insurance company was covering their additional living expenses. Unlike their house in town, this house was fresh and clean. Their belongings were organized. I praised Amber for the way she had set up her household.

I was hopeful.

But over time Amber rarely answered her phone when I called. Ron and I would drive out to their country home and find it a mess. Jesse slept on the couch, while Amber rushed to tidy the house, embarrassed to look us in the eyes. Years later, we learned what Jake and Cyndi had observed at least once when they went to visit: both Amber and Jesse in a drugged stupor, asleep in bed. Jake and Cyndi had taken the kids home for a while until their parents finally awoke and came for them.

Ron and I didn't know Amber and Jesse were using drugs. Looking back, I don't know if we were naïve or didn't want to face it. We had suspected marijuana; I had seen ashes; and I had seen empty Adderall® capsules in their house, but we didn't know the reality of it all. All I knew was that my daughter was falling deep into a pit of despair, and I felt helpless.

Ron and I fervently prayed for Amber and Jesse and their children. We prayed together. We prayed alone. We asked our friends and church family to pray. I knew God loved me and desired to answer my prayer that Amber would turn back to the Lord God she had called upon when she was a little girl. But I didn't see my prayer answered, and I wondered why. I did see answers to one of my greatest prayers—the children were still protected.

I thanked God. I trusted Him, but trusting Him didn't come easily to me while answers were not forthcoming. I struggled and had to commit her to the LORD, repeatedly, day after day. Certainly He was faithful even when Amber was not. And because of His faithfulness, I was still hopeful.

And Jesus Whispered ~

Be joyful in your hope. Be patient in this affliction. Be faithful in your prayer.

Ron and I were not the only family members affected by the drug demons in Amber's and Jesse's lives. Amber's brother Matt and sister-in-law Lynette were also concerned. Matt, an insurance agent, recognized that Amber and Jesse were making poor decisions with their insurance company in handling the details of their claim for the fire. He knew they were wasting insurance money instead of using it to their advantage to get back on their feet and back into their house. Lynette was frustrated with the way Amber neglected our family. Matt and Lynette drove three hours from their home to gather with us all for family events and holidays. Sometimes Amber and Jesse were late; other times they never came. The cousins were disappointed. We were all disappointed. Easter, Thanksgiving, Christmas, birthday parties. Every occasion was stressful.

Has Amber called? Are they coming? Should we go ahead and eat dinner without them?

One of the biggest disappointments in our family time occurred every summer during our family vacation week at a beautiful Christian resort on Lake Michigan. Ron and I rented a cottage for a week every summer, and our older kids planned their vacation time around it. The children attended classes and made crafts, while we adults attended sessions led by great speakers. Praise and worship saturated the place! Our afternoons were spent on the beach or at the pool. We were making great memories, but Amber and Jesse chose not to be a part of those memories. Occasionally they came for an overnight, usually on their way elsewhere. One summer, Ron and I took Jacob, Benny, and Kaylee with us. Amber had said she would join us the next day, but she never came at all that week. We all loved having the children with us, but we wanted Amber and Jesse there, too, and so did their children.

Amber's sister Kristen and her husband Josh were also troubled by what was going on with Amber and Jesse. Josh had suggested job opportunities to Jesse, but Jesse had not pursued any of them. Amber didn't answer Kristen's phone calls. The two sisters, once close, rarely spoke. Matt and Lynette and Kristen and Josh were diligent in their prayers and were faithful in loving their younger sister; nonetheless, tension pervaded our entire family.

Not only did tension arise in our family but it also surfaced in Jesse's extended family. Jesse's brother and sister were greatly concerned over Amber and Jesse's drug use, again a drug use our family suspected but had not evidenced. Jesse's parents Jake and Cyndi were devastated as well and had reached the end of their rope with their son and Amber. They believed Jesse and Amber had to hit "rock bottom" before they would change. I was praying for deliverance before they hit the depths. Then tragedy hit Jesse's family and devastated us all.

FACING the THIEF

> *The thief comes only to steal and kill and destroy. John 10:10*

In July, Jesse's mom Cyndi suffered an undiagnosed pain that didn't go away. Jake took her to a specialist who discovered an advanced stage of pancreatic cancer. By January, she had passed. Beautiful, vibrant Cyndi was gone. My heart ached. I had known Cyndi since high school days. I remembered her as a pretty young woman. Then I had lost contact with her until our Amber started dating her Jesse. Though years had passed, I still saw her as the cute young girl she had been. Her heart was full of love for her husband, Jake, her children, and for her grandchildren—the grandchildren we now shared. When Cyndi passed away, I was filled with sadness, especially for my grandchildren who had lost their other Nana. I held those children closely and prayed I could be faithful for them and to them.

Ron and I reached out to Jake and the family as much as we could. We hoped to show Christ to them, to be His hands, His feet, and His arms of love. We had drawn close to Jesse's family during those months before Cyndi's passing. We were at the hospital, praying, and saying our goodbyes an hour before she went to heaven. But Jesse, her own son, was not. It was not because he didn't care. I knew he loved his mother immensely. I had observed that love through the thirteen years I had known Jesse. But now, the ugly demon tormenting Jesse demanded Jesse's attention. The demon enemy does that. It laughs at pain and suffering.

It laughed at me two days later. And it made me cry.

One evening, before the funeral, Ron and I had gone to Jake's house to be with his family, including the extended family. I sat in the living room, talking to a family member. In his grief, this man was drunk and blubbered repeatedly about how sad Jesse and Amber's situation was—how the drugs had ruined them – how he thought their house fire had actually started. I was puzzled.

Jesse and Amber on drugs? How did he know this? Jake and Cyndi had told him but not told us? Did he not know of the Fire Marshal's report?

As I looked at Jesse's sweet Christian Grandma sitting near me, I suspected my transparent face must have exposed my bewilderment. Her face revealed heartache for me and showed that she too was puzzled by what she heard. The atmosphere in the room was suddenly oppressive. I stood and stepped out of it. I would give the enemy no more contentment in causing me pain.

But in the midst of the sorrow of death and the uncertainty we were all experiencing, a light was shining through the darkness. This light was the Light of the World.[2] It never burns out. It shines through the darkness and can light up an entire family! And that light is stronger than the demon enemy who delivers pain, hate, agony, lies, and suffering. Yes, that light was shining through the darkness, and it touched the heart of Jake and his family.

When you are in the dark, listen, and God will give you a very precious message.
~Oswald Chambers

Cyndi had accepted the Lord Jesus as her Savior when she was younger and in her last months we could sense her reaching out to her family with the good news of Jesus the Son of God who died on the cross for our sins, rose from the grave, ascended into heaven, and sits at the right hand of the Father. Cyndi wanted her family reunited and whole again. Jake, Jesse, his sister, Angela, and his brother, Matt, all knew that Cyndi wanted the love of Jesus Christ to cover their family.

When Cyndi passed away, Jake reached out to the one man who could comfort him and give him spiritual guidance—his old fishing buddy, Chaplain Dave. Chaplain Dave was a family friend who had accompanied Jake and his young boys on fishing trips. Chaplain Dave had shared the good news of the Lord Jesus with Jake many times, and each time Jake was interested but not interested enough. Chaplain Dave was patient. Now, Jake asked Chaplain Dave to hold Cyndi's funeral. Chaplain Dave offered his home church. Hundreds of people attended. Jesse sat beside his dad, his arm around his dad's shoulder, in tender comfort. Not only was the sunlight shining through the church windows that day, but the Light of the World was manifesting Himself, also. Jake's heart opened to the message of the LORD Jesus. In the days and weeks following the funeral, he began meeting with Chaplain Dave. One day, Jake prayed to receive Jesus Christ as his Savior, and Jake was so excited about his newfound faith, he began to share his good news with everyone, including us. The Light of the World connected our two families.

And Jesus Whispered ~

I am the light of the world. Whoever follows me will never walk in darkness but will have the light of life.

Now I was truly hopeful.

Because of the difficulties with the insurance agency and since he had no job, Jesse decided to finish the repair work on the fire-damaged house himself. This decision was one of the best he had ever made. He hung drywall and cabinets, installed electricity and plumbing, and completed the finishing work. His house was done, and the work was approved by inspectors. We commended Jesse for a job well done. The house was beautiful and clean. A relative offered gently-used furniture. The family moved back in, and we all helped them get settled! It was a fresh start.

Again, I was hopeful.

But Amber did not have a job, and once again, Jesse was unfaithful to his job. With time on their hands, they lay in bed or on the couch much of the day. Jacob, their oldest child, fended for himself and took on many responsibilities for the younger children. We heard rumors of the children roaming the neighborhood alone. The dog chewed the woodwork and the window blinds and brought fleas into the house. The newly refurbished home soon became a pit of filth—this time, worse than before.

Much had changed in my life. This was supposed to be a time of looking toward retirement, a time Ron and I could vacation and travel. Our children were supposed to be independent and self-sufficient. But Amber and Jesse were neither independent nor self-sufficient.

Even more life-changing, a spiritual battle was taking place. Ron and I were at war with the enemy, the thief. He was stealing and killing and destroying our family,[3] right in front of our eyes. The Word of God is *truth,* and it told me about the enemy:

> *"But while everyone was sleeping, his enemy came and sowed weeds among the wheat, and went away."*
>
> *"Where then did the weeds come from?"*
>
> *"An enemy did this," he replied.*
>
> *"The weeds are the sons of the evil one, and the enemy who sows them is the devil."[4]*

Our battle was against the enemy, the devil. I had the power to fight back. I was in the Lord's army. So I put on the armor.

FACING the ENEMY in OUR DAUGHTER'S DEFENSE
It had been Paul's final instructions to the Ephesians: *"Finally, be strong in the LORD and in his mighty power. Put on the full armor of God*

so that you can take your stand against the devil's schemes. For our struggle is not against flesh and blood, but against the rulers, against the authorities, against the powers of this dark world and against the spiritual forces of evil in the heavenly realms. Therefore put on the full armor of God, so that when the day of evil comes, you may be able to stand your ground, and after you have done everything, to stand."[5]

The instructions were given to the church members in Ephesus, and to me. The passage continued, "Stand firm then, with the belt of truth buckled around your waist."[6]

I know the truth. Jesus is the truth. His Word is truth.

Earlier in his letter, Paul had told the Ephesians to "speak the truth in love."[7] These instructions confirmed the exact path I had been taking to reach my daughter, the path to break through the evil force that was surrounding her. It was a path of love.

I had carried her within me, and I had loved her from that time. Her backsliding didn't change my love for her. Her anger or harsh words didn't change my love for her. I flooded her with unending love.

The instructions Paul gave to the Ephesians and to me are the inspired Word of God. The passage continued speaking of *righteousness* and *readiness* and *faith:* "With the breastplate of righteousness in place, and with your feet fitted with the readiness that comes from the gospel of peace. In addition to all this, take up the shield of faith, with which you can extinguish all the flaming arrows of the evil one."[8]

28

I want this faith. I need this faith. And with this faith, I can extinguish all the flaming arrows of the evil one.

The final piece of armor? The sword! The sword of the Spirit! God's Word! "Take the helmet of salvation and the sword of the Spirit, which is the word of God."[9] I delved into it; I searched it; it became more alive to me than it had ever been. "Consequently, faith comes from hearing the message, and the message is heard through the word of Christ."[10]

My faith will increase through hearing the Word!

I pictured myself with the armor—the belt, the breastplate, the footwear, the helmet—with a shield in one hand and my Bible in the other. Yes, I put on the armor, and I pictured the Lord God Almighty, the Most High leading me, surrounding me, filling me, protecting me, and delivering me and my beautiful daughter, Amber.

Trusting Him didn't come easy for me during that time. Fears came. Often. I had to keep reading the Word and speaking the Word. The Word, itself, became my prayer to Him: Lord, *you have said that because you love me, you will rescue me; because you love Amber; you will rescue her. I will call upon you, and you will answer me. You will be with me in trouble; you will deliver me and will honor me! My, what a gracious and awesome God you are!*[11]

And Jesus Whispered ~

Kathi, I made you and I know you. I give you understanding of my Word. Someday Amber will rejoice because you have put your hope in my Word.

I came to realize the amazing power in the Word of God, and as I did, God led me to share His Word with Amber. I began writing letters to her. I wrote two or three times a week, occasionally including a few dollars or perhaps a ten-dollar bill, hoping to entice her to gather her mail from the box and to open the next letter I would send. I envisioned her *receiving* the Word of God in her home, thus disturbing the enemy; should she open the letter and *read* the Word, the power would permeate her house; and should she *pray* the Word, well, I couldn't imagine. I knew the power of God's Word, "For the word of God is living and active. Sharper than any double-edged sword, it penetrates even to dividing soul and spirit, joints and marrow; it judges the thoughts and attitudes of the heart."[12]

Father God, penetrate my Amber's soul, with your mighty Word.

My letters, such as the one below, included pleasant small talk and then an encouragement to pray God's Word:

Dear Amber,

I hope you all had a good weekend. The weather was nice, wasn't it? Dad's face and neck are sunburned. My nose got red. Friday wasn't sunny, but it was sunny all day Saturday, and we were out in it all day.

This morning, I sat out on my porch. It's raining and 64 degrees, but I enjoyed the solitude while reading from the Psalms. Here are some verses I prayed, and I ask you to pray with me, Amber. Let God's Word work its awesome power in you, Amber. Find a quiet place now and pray His Word.

"I ascribe to you, Lord, the glory due your name. Your voice is powerful and majestic.[13] I exalt you, O Lord, for you lift me out of the depths and do not let my enemies gloat over me. I call to you for help, and you heal me. You spare me from going down into the pit. Your anger lasts only a moment, but your favor lasts a lifetime![14] In you, O Lord, I take refuge. Let me never be put to shame; deliver me in your righteousness. Turn your ear to me; come quickly to my rescue. Into your hands I commit my spirit. You see my affliction and know the anguish of my soul. Be merciful to me, O Lord, for I am in distress; my strength fails. But I trust in you, O Lord; I say, 'You are my God.' Let your face shine

on your servant; save me in your unfailing love. How great is your goodness which you have stored up for those who fear you."[15]

His word is our Power.

Love, Mom

As the Holy Spirit led, I wrote more letters. My letters to Amber were positive and cheerful, but because I didn't always feel positive and cheerful, I sometimes wrote letters that, after proofreading, I didn't mail.

Dear Amber,

I hope this printed letter doesn't seem impersonal — it might be the most personal I've written to you yet. I can get my ideas down on paper quicker by keyboarding than handwriting. I was awake most of the night, worrying and praying for you and your family. Today, I am not selecting the next passage in my Bible reading. Instead, specific verses come to my mind, and I will share them with you.

Amber, you must get yourself up out of this pit of despair. You have delved into things which have allowed the enemy to get a hold on you. It has changed you. Now you must turn from it. The Bible tells us that "No one who is born of God will continue to sin."[16]

You are not alone, Amber. God will give you all the strength you need, and certainly Dad and I will help you. "You, dear children, are from God and have overcome them every spirit that is not from God, because the one who is in you is greater than the one who is in the world"[17]

You must "drive out (these) demons by the Spirit of God, then the kingdom of God has come upon you"[18] Rebuke the enemy, Amber. Say it aloud. Bind the enemy. Tell the enemy to leave your home in the name of Jesus; the enemy has no power over you, Jesse, Jacob, Ben, Kaylee, or your home. Ask the Holy Spirit to fill you, Jesse, and your home. Forbid the enemy to be there. Rid your home of anything you know is dark or sinful. Take your children out of your home, if you feel you need to. I will get help for you. Call Kristen and Josh to come and pray over you and Jesse and your home, if you want. Call Dad and me if you want.

There is a great chasm, Amber, dividing the right and light side from the dark side. You must choose the right side. Who is your King? We read about this chasm in Luke 16:19-31 and Matthew 12:28-37.

What do you want your children to remember about their childhood?

"If we confess our sins, he is faithful and just and will forgive us our sins and purify us from all un-righteousness. If we claim we have no sin, we make him out to be a liar and his Word has no place in our lives"[19]

I want you to talk to me about this. I want you to call me, I want you to let me know what you plan to do.

Love, Mom

I want . . . I want . . . I want. In proofreading, I sometimes found my letters were filled with *self* instead of *Jesus*. So I tore those letters into pieces. *Self* instead of *Jesus*. Now I could see it vividly. So many times I had shown *self* to friends and family instead of showing *Jesus*. I often had tried to arrange, oversee, direct, or manipulate so many situations in the lives of my friends and family. It was not easy for me now to trust God to work in Amber's life. But I tried to trust. I confessed *self*, and I prayed.

On my knees, day after day, I pleaded with the Lord Jesus to intercede to the Father in behalf of Amber and her family. I depended on the Word: "but because Jesus lives forever . . . he is able to save completely those who come to God through him, because he always lives to intercede for them."[20]

The Word—my Lord Jesus—was alive. He was interceding for me.

> *For this is what the LORD says—he who created the heavens, he is God. . . "I am the LORD, and there is no other. I have not spoken in secret, from somewhere in a land of darkness . . . I, the LORD, speak the truth; I declare what is right"* (Isaiah 45:18, 19).

"I have not spoken in secret," the LORD says. "I speak the truth."[21] In the midst of my storm, His Word revealed truth to me.

In her book *Wounded by God's People* Anne Graham Lotz shares personal experiences of being "storm-tossed and not comforted." She suggests her readers "take a deep breath," and consider, "Could it be that you have not been listening to God's voice? Really listening, with your eyes on the pages of your Bible. I have no doubt that He is right there beside you." I wanted to really listen. Through delving into His Word, the Bible, listening to the whisper of His voice, and setting my eyes on the pages of my Bible, I discovered truth. The truths in His Word helped me to truly understand the amazing grace of God, the grace He promises, and the grace that proves to be sufficient. In His Word, Jesus whispered to me of this grace.

And Jesus Whispered ~

Trust me, Kathi. No one loves Amber more than I do—not Jesse, not Ron, and not even you. My Word is truth. Remain in it. Remain in me.

1. At the beginning of this chapter, I quoted the well-known preacher, Charles Spurgeon: "Take care you know what the Holy Ghost teaches. Do not give way to a faint-hearted ignorance, lest you be great losers thereby." It was much easier for Ron and me to be ignorant of our daughter's drug use than to face it head on. Facing the demon was terrifying. How have you had to face evil in your life or in the life of a loved one in order for the truth to be revealed?

Read John 16: 12-15. Reflect upon how you can learn truth from the Holy Spirit, the "Spirit of truth."

Next, read John 14:16-17(a) and 14:26. What does Jesus say the Counselor will do? How do you think the Counselor "reminds you" of everything Jesus said?

2. In his book, Everyday Blessings: 365 Days of Inspirational Thoughts, Max Lucado writes, "The next time you find yourself alone in a dark alley facing the undeniables of life . . . be still, whisper His name, and listen. He is nearer than you think." Many of us have been in this dark alley alone, facing trials we didn't want or expect. Consider your own experiences in the past, a trial you are now facing, or a hypothetical situation. What are the benefits or blessings of being still, whispering His name, and listening when facing those "undeniables of life"?

3. In this chapter, I wrote that we are instructed to "put on the full armor of God,"[22] which includes the "belt of truth,"[23] and that we must "speak the truth in love"[24] to others we love. Read Ephesians 4:20-32 and 2 Timothy 2:15-16 and 24-26. What traits do we find in one who speaks the truth in love?

4. I quoted Anne Graham Lotz who challenges us to question if we are listening to God's voice—"Really listening, with your eyes on the pages of your Bible." To what or to whom do you listen? Where are your eyes looking? On the pages of the Bible, God's Word? Or elsewhere? What do these verses tell us about His Word: John 17: 15-17 and Psalm 119, particularly verses 11, 37, 74, 105, 130, 133?

chapter two

Whispers of Grace

Dealing with Disappointment by Grasping His Grace

Grace is the voice that calls us to change
and then gives us the power to pull it off.
~MAX LUCADO

As the Apostle Paul begins his letter to Christians in Colossae, he writes about truth and grace. He commends the Colossians for their "faith in Christ Jesus" and for their "love for all of God's people," which came from the "confident hope" stored up for them in heaven.[25] Those reading the letter had already heard about that hope in the "word of truth, the gospel," which was bearing fruit and growing all over the world as it was among them since the day they first "heard it and understood God's grace in all its truth."[26] Now I looked back on my life and began to recognize how God's grace had grown in me. I was understanding His grace in all its truth.

"His grace is sufficient for thee!"[27] Those words were engraved on the plaque on my bedroom wall as I grew up, a plaque I had earned in Vacation Bible School at the little country church our family attended. As a child, I had learned, memorized, and recited the verse. As time passed, I heard it quoted by preachers, Sunday School teachers, and others who offered advice. I read about grace in the Bible—*saving* grace, totally undeserved. So from those early days, I believed in that grace, although I hadn't yet begun to grasp its fullness. As time went on, I began to learn that His grace had not only *saved* me but was *teaching* me, as well: "For the grace of God that brings salvation has appeared to all men. It teaches us to say, 'No' to ungodliness and worldly passions, and to live self-controlled, upright and godly lives in this present age."[28]

Jesus was whispering messages of grace to me, and I continued to listen to those whispers.

Grasping His Grace in My Broken Career

When Ron and I opened North Woods Coffee Co., I had intended to continue teaching at the local high school. We assumed I would only work the business on the weekends. But on the summer day we opened, we both knew I would have to leave my teaching position. The business was much larger than we had expected, and it required both of our full-time efforts. When I resigned my teaching position, my principal assured me that whenever I wanted to return, he would hire me back into the school system. He said I had ten years of positive experience in the district, and my love for my students was obvious to all. Three years later, about mid-way through our business ownership, a position opened at the high school, a position nearly identical to the one I had held. Financially, I needed the position. Physically, it seemed like a relief to go back to teaching after the exhausting work at the store. And of course, I loved teaching! So I applied and was interviewed by my former peers and the principal, the principal who had promised to rehire me. Instead, he hired another person from outside the area. She taught only one year and then moved on to another school. The position was reposted. This time, I included even more credentials with my application. But, I was not called for an interview. The position was given to someone else, again from outside the school district. It was a hard pill to swallow.

In the last two months of our business ownership, our daughter Kristen having given birth to her first child, Noah, took a maternity leave from her teaching position in our nearby hometown school district. At her recommendation, I was hired for the long-term sub position for her 7th grade Language Arts class, which was nearly identical to a class I had taught for many years. The two-month substitute position was a positive experience and came naturally to me. I gave it 200%, going well beyond the expectations of a temporary teacher. Kristen returned to work, completing the last few weeks of the school year. Shortly thereafter she turned in her resignation, deciding to be home with her son. In the summer, her position was posted in the district, and I applied for it. By this time we had sold North Woods Coffee Co., and I was anxious to get back to full-time teaching. I was confident it was the Lord's leading that I get the position and certain that the principal was pleased with the work I had done. Sure enough, I was called for a first interview. However I was not called for a second interview; another person from outside the district was granted the position.

Within the next years I applied for several more openings within local districts, all to no avail. I was humiliated. By this time I was teaching as adjunct faculty at two colleges. As my college experience increased and my résumé expanded, I applied at community colleges throughout the state, sending dozens of résumés and making follow-up calls on each but always with no response and no request for an interview. I yearned for an office at a college. I was humbled, but even more I felt demeaned. I began to look at life and people differently. I was now keenly aware of every negative comment made about unemployed people. I took those comments personally. Powerless to find a position, I often felt defeated. But a part of the armor I carried was the sword, the Word of God, and that Word told me that God loved me. I only needed to trust Him. He gave me the grace to do it.

"He giveth more grace when the burdens grow greater." It was an old hymn I had heard and had sung for many years. As a young woman I knew that one day, perhaps years later, trials would come, and so I wanted to grow strong in His grace, strong enough to depend totally upon God when I needed Him most. Now at this time of my life my burdens *had* become greater, and it wasn't only because of the troubles my daughter was experiencing or my disappointments in not having a full-time job. I also watched my precious Mama's and Daddy's health decline.

GRASPING HIS GRACE in MY OWN HELPLESSNESS

I especially began to understand and depend upon God's grace while caring for my Mama and Daddy. Years before, Ron and I had bought a chunk of land on my parents' farm and had built a home next door to them. It was in this home and the surrounding property that we raised our children. They scurried back and forth across the yards to Grandma and Grandpa's house, each time learning a lesson about nature or family values. As the years passed, we realized the amazing legacy Mama and Daddy had given us, not only in the land, but in the Lord. This legacy had begun with two young people who gave themselves to the Lord, then to each other, and now had passed the legacy to us and to our children.

As a child, my mother Margie lived in a small white farmhouse two miles from the little country church in Butler Township. On Sundays she, along with her brothers and sisters, sauntered the dry gravel roads to church. The parade of children was led by the stern and proper matriarch of the family, Grandma Locke. She lived with the family, as was often the custom in the first half of the 20th century.

My father Wayne was one of an even larger batch of children. He lived twenty miles away in Ovid Township in a yet smaller weathered farmhouse. On Sunday mornings, in contrast to Margie, Wayne walked alone the dry gravel roads that turned wet in the rain or icy in the winter. Wayne met up with a traveling pastor who faithfully drove from Ovid Township on Sunday mornings and evenings to preach at the little country church, Dayburg Baptist Church, in Butler Township. In and around that quaint little building with its grassy churchyard, Margie and her siblings met young Wayne. The Locke family took to Wayne, which led to him spending long Sunday afternoons with them at their country home. Late in the day, after the Sunday evening service, Wayne rode with the pastor back to Ovid Township and walked the short mile home. Wayne's friendship developed with the Locke family, and especially with cute little Margie. One summer afternoon the young couple crossed the creek behind the church and ambled through the woods. Wayne carved their initials, connected by an arrow, into the trunk of a young tree: W N + M L. By the time Wayne graduated from Coldwater High School, the United States had entered the Second World

War. He signed up and served overseas for three years. Oh how he missed the country church and his sweet Margie! Margie worked in a factory, helping the war effort. Those years dragged. The young couple corresponded, and their letters spoke of love and of marriage. In 1946, after the war had ended and Wayne returned home, he and Margie were married at the little country church, just a short distance from that carved tree in the woods.

They bought a farm near that woods behind the church where they had wandered. The creek where they had both been baptized bordered their farm on the south. The beautiful yellow farmhouse sat on the hill, midway to the northern property line. It was a house Margie had admired since she walked the dusty roads as a child. Her dream had come true. Wayne and Margie served the LORD together in the little country church and the surrounding community. They raised their family in the yellow farmhouse.

The legacy had begun with my parents. Now they had aged, and as a result my life was changing. Faithfulness was a Christ-like trait I had observed in my parents, and I wanted to demonstrate it, in return, to them. I determined to be faithful to them until the end. I picked up the shield of faith, and as I did, God's grace covered me and strengthened me.

My mother had been a stronghold in my life as I grew up. I witnessed in her a resilient woman who was unwavering in her Christian walk and in the care of her family. She loved her home and kept it clean and tidy. She loved the land and maintained a huge garden, canning and freezing everything she could grow. She had such a heart for people. One day I walked in the house and smelled a large pot of chili on the stove. "Who's this for?" I asked, suspecting she was giving it to someone in the neighborhood.

"It's for the Andrews family," she replied.

"But they don't go to our church!"

"Well, they need to eat, don't they?" she responded. I don't know if Mr. Andrews was out of work, or if Mrs. Andrews was ill at the time. But I knew they and their five kids wouldn't go hungry that night.

As a teenager I wondered why Mama didn't get her teeth fixed. When I matured I realized it was because she was working for my prom dresses and other fringes. She was a busy, productive woman who worked a difficult factory job every day, yet never missed Thursday night prayer meetings. If she was ever ill, I never knew it.

Now that she had aged, Mama's health had declined. She became depressed, often taking out her frustrations on me. God's grace covered me. I watched her body change from upright to bent. From solid to stumbling. From standing to falling. From being happy to faking happy. She went through tests, invasive procedures, painful treatments, multiple diagnoses, and enormous doses of medications. Her already purpled thin skin was often battered and bandaged. Her bones fractured. But in spite of her broken body, God evidenced his grace in her spirit. Seeing that grace imparted to her made me embrace His grace as well, knowing it was sufficient, just as I had learned as a child.

Daddy was a godly man. He exemplified Christ's love for the church in his love for my Mama. He represented the Heavenly Father's love to me. He was compassionate, and he showed love to people. I loved him for it. In his younger years, he led the youth group at our small country church. Dozens of children grew closer to the Lord because of Daddy's teaching. Later, in his years before retirement, Daddy took his vacation time from work to counsel at Camp Selah, a Christian camp for children. His feet were the feet of Christ and His arms were the Father's arms to many broken children and to people throughout our community.

Daddy worked a full-time office job but spent evenings and Saturdays working on the land and cutting wood for the furnace to heat the big yellow house in the cold winters. Daddy loved nature and planted thousands of pine trees on the farm so the animals would have a place of refuge. Near the creek, he created a beautiful picnic area where we held family reunions and church picnics.

God's grace was evidenced in Daddy's life, as in Mama's life, as dementia slowly assaulted his frail body and his honorable mind. He had enjoyed mowing his lawn, spending hours on his John Deere lawn tractor, wearing his old straw hat! It was a pleasant and familiar sight, one I had cherished for years. One day, I noticed he mowed his lawn in a maze of pathways. Later, with a puzzled smile on his face, he sat on the green seat of his John Deere unaware of how to start it or how to adjust its mowing deck. Soon, he was making odd statements, and seeing strange sights, things I didn't repeat to others, for the sake of his dignity. The vile dementia had attacked my precious Daddy, but through it all, his heart stayed loving and his spirit stayed sweet. God's grace was a fine mist over Daddy and over me.

Then the day came when my brother and I had to take Daddy to a nursing home. I had fought it, and I didn't want to face it. I had never considered the idea of either Mama or Daddy going to a nursing home. None of my grandparents had gone to nursing homes, so I assumed neither of my parents would. But Mama's health had declined to the point that she could no longer care for Daddy, and my home wasn't safe enough for him. He needed 24-hour care. It was the most difficult decision I had ever made. I awoke early on that day we were to take him.

I'm going next door to get Daddy's clothing. I'll bring him here to my house. I'm not taking him to the nursing home.

But questions entered my mind. They were questions I needed to face. They were questions of reality: *Who will be with him when I go to work? How will I keep him from wandering outside? From leaving the yard? From going near the swimming pool?*

I faced my questions, and I hated the answers they brought. And so we took him. The sting of separation punctured so sharply that my brother and I could hardly look at each other, for fear we would break down in front of Daddy. It wasn't until we left the facility that we sobbed like babies. Daddy's babies. Time and age had no bearing on this matter. I hated this dementia and its attack on my Daddy, how it was separating him from my Mama, and the sadness it brought our family. But as He steadily does in both easy times and agonizing times, the warm shower of God's grace covered my Mama, my brother and me, and my Daddy.

Of course, it was hardest on Mama. But a relief. Not that Daddy was away from the house but that now she could let go. Mama had several debilitating diseases, and she was worn out from fighting them. I encouraged her to continue in a gift God had given her: prayer. I reminded her that I needed her prayers and my children needed her prayers. And now, although she was faithful to pray, she didn't want to stay. Mama had loved, honored, and served Daddy for 65 years, but now that he was being cared for in the nursing home, she felt her work on Earth was finished. He was safe and protected, so she released herself to her disease. She was too weak to go on.

My encouragement didn't seem to help. Mama asked to go to the same nursing home. We waited for an opening, and while we waited, I begged Mama to live with Ron and me. She would have her own bedroom and bathroom. I was convinced it could work out. "You can sit on my back porch, Mom, and look right across the yard at your own home. You can watch the deer and the wild turkeys like you've always done." But I couldn't persuade her. So when the call came that the nursing home had an opening, Mama accepted it. The next morning, my sister and I took Mama. It was a hard day for us. My heart was broken. It was not my desire, but I respected Mama's wishes.

The staff at the nursing home loved my parents. I knew they saw Jesus in each of them. I visited my mother and father several times a week, arranging and sorting their clothing, taking Daddy's plaid flannel shirts home to iron, and helping Mama with her daily tasks. It was a beautiful, clean medical care facility, and we were thankful both Mama and Daddy could live there. Because of Daddy's dementia, he was in a special, charming unit of the facility, and Mama was in the adjoining lovely unit. She could visit him every day. Each time I returned home from visiting them, I drove in my driveway and looked across the yards at their home. The yellow house. Its emptiness entered me.

Sometimes in the morning, I took a cup of coffee and sat on my south porch, facing their house, the house where I had grown up, the house where Daddy and Mama had lived most of their 65 years together. No matter the season, it now looked cold and lonely. In those latter years, the meager Social Security income hadn't allowed improvements on the house or the surrounding property. Dementia and crippling disease had also stifled its maintenance and had cloned themselves into the structure of the house itself. As Daddy and Mama had wearied, so had the house. It cracked and creaked and sagged. Its outside was worn, sun bleached, and peeling. Like Daddy's and Mama's faces, its face revealed its loss of hope. Utility bills, property taxes, and insurance premiums continued to fill the mailbox every month. The social security income was now transferred to the nursing home. The yellow house had lost its caretakers and now its nourishment. It was dying. Reality set in. The house faced it and so did I: Daddy and Mama wouldn't be coming home. This time, God's grace was a bit difficult to unearth, but in time, I found it, or shall I say, it found me!

Caring for elderly parents is stressful to anyone, especially when one is bearing other burdens, as well. I was fortunate that my brother and sister were loving and faithful to Mama and Daddy, and they joined me in visiting them often in the nursing home and attending to their needs. Daddy had to have surgery. He also battled infections. Mama fell and broke her hip. The re-constructive surgery was unsuccessful. Three weeks later, she had a second surgery. My heart ached for both of them. Watching my parents suffer was heartbreaking.

In addition, most of the responsibilities of maintaining the yellow house and the surrounding two-acres were mine. Work needed to be done, and I had to do it: Mowing lawns. Trimming bushes. Cleaning the house. Sorting a lifelong household of belongings. It was tiring, and I was already worn. But I held my sword, the Word of God, and I listened to Jesus.

And Jesus Whispered ~

Come to me, Kathi, for you are weary and burdened. I will give you rest. Take my yoke upon you and learn from me, for I am gentle and humble in heart, and you will find rest for your soul. For my yoke is easy and my burden is light.

In spite of his dementia, Daddy was loving. He knew me and was always pleased to see me. I cherished our visits and loved snuggling his neck with my cheeks. He didn't know I was struggling with other issues. My mother, on the other hand, was perceptive and discerning, and she could read me like a book. While she lived in her home next door, I had trouble hiding our distress over Amber, but now that Mama was in the nursing home, it was easier for me to keep her from knowing our troubles. She was suffering her own physical ailments, and she didn't need any added burdens.

And the truth was, by this time, Ron and I were fighting the biggest battle of our lives in this struggle against the enemy for our Amber. I didn't know how, nor was I emotionally able to cover up Amber's problems every time her grandma asked about her, so I pacified my Mama with simple answers and learned to quickly change the subject. I did this, not for my own sake but because I wanted my Mama to be as comfortable as possible. This close, strong, lifelong relationship with my parents seemed to intensify my inner pain and my feelings of helplessness, but my relationship with the Lord, or perhaps I should say, His relationship with me, granted the grace to get through it.

GRASPING HIS GRACE in MY WOUNDED MARRIAGE

Many years previous, shortly after Ron and I were married in my little home church, the doors of the church closed. Nothing would ever be the same there again. But as my mother and father had grown close to the Lord within one country church, Ron and I would do the same at another. Rev. Clyde Mills, an evangelical pastor of East Algansee Baptist Church, a vibrant church south of Quincy had shared the gospel message with Ron before we were married, and Ron had eagerly accepted the Lord Jesus as his Savior. It was some years before I realized the tremendous favor God had shown to us. We developed great friendships with other young Christian couples at our church, and we were all starving for a closer relationship with our Lord, so we studied the Word and grew in faith. Those were good years. Ron and I loved the Lord God together and wanted to honor Him. Our children were active in AWANA and youth groups. Ron served on the church board and was a Sunday School teacher. I played the piano, led the choir and sometimes taught a Sunday School class.

Matt graduated from high school, went to college, and married Lynette. By that time, Kristen was in college, and Amber was still a young teenager at home. She was lonely for her brother and sister. She seemed unhappy. As a little girl, Amber had accepted Jesus as her Savior, but now she didn't want to talk about the Lord and didn't want to read her Bible. Unlike her older sister and brother, Amber wanted to keep to herself around the house. Things were different, and I wondered if Ron and I were actually to blame. When Amber was seven years old, I began a Bachelor degree program, and by the time she was eleven, I was teaching full time. Ron was busy establishing his new business in semi parts and service. We loved and nurtured Amber through her teen years. After high school, she was accepted at college, but instead, she wanted to get married. So we gave her a beautiful wedding ceremony, and little Jacob, our first grandchild, was born the next year. Ron and I had passed our Christian heritage on to our children; and now to our grandchildren. Soon we were blessed with many grandchildren.

But throughout our marriage, we had carried a problem that had developed within the first years. It was private, it was divisive, and it was destructive. Time after time, we discussed it. We sought counseling; but the problem was never gone. It hung like a weight around my neck. I held a grudge and resentment. I was wrong to do that. The voice and tone I used with my husband evidenced my bitterness. The problem was fueled by strife with our extended family and by unemployment and by the normal stressors of life. Throughout the years, we masked it. We covered it with smiles and hugs, but the problem kept breaking through the façade. Any outside tension stirred the coals and created new flames. I inwardly blamed Ron's parenting for Amber's resultant wayward life, and occasionally I let him know it, either directly or by my responses and reactions to him. Again, I could relate to the prophet Elijah. Both before and after the tumult, the Lord asked Elijah what he was doing in the cave, an obvious inference that God had not led Elijah to the cave. Elijah responded with complaining and excuses: "I have been very zealous for the Lord God Almighty. The Israelites have rejected your covenant, broken down your altars, and put your prophets to death with the sword. I am the only one left, and now they are trying to kill me too."[29]

As Elijah complained about the Israelites and blamed them for rejecting God's covenant and doing wrong, I complained about Ron and blamed him for our problems. As Elijah felt alone and undeservedly chastised, I felt alone and undeservedly chastised. I believed myself to be the *right* and *zealous* one in our marriage. Instead, I needed to confess and forgive. I needed to get away from the enemy's control of my emotions. And so I prayed constantly about it, and finally, grace took the place of my excuses. I spoke my love for Ron to God and to Ron. I prayed, thanking God for Ron. God's grace covered me. Many painful memories disappeared, and as other unpleasant memories surfaced, I was able to rebuke them by quoting God's word. I learned to replace them with good memories, memories Ron and I created together. Ruth Bell Graham once said, "A happy marriage is the union of two good forgivers." I knew I was responsible to be *one* of those "good forgivers" in my marriage. Ron and I found solutions that equipped both of us to serve God in our home and in our jobs. We worked together to make one another better.

Although I was raised in a Christian home and knew that I was saved by God's grace, I grew into adulthood not recognizing that I was made the righteousness of God in Jesus Christ.[30] Guilt over past and present sins was ever present. Condemnation haunted me. I thought God would punish my every sin. I tried to *become* holy, not realizing that I was already *made* holy through the finished work of Christ. It was frustrating and created bouts of depression.

When our children were grown, I faced many regrets. I wished I had spent more time playing with Matt, had given Kristen piano lessons, and had attended more of Amber's school activities. Friends spoke of similar regrets, so I hoped it was natural, but later, when Amber's life was literally falling apart, I had to question my part in it. People made comments, such as "You raise them all the same, but sometimes one turns out differently than the others!" Deep inside, I knew that Ron and I had *not* raised our three children all the same. Although we had instilled the same values and had taught them all about the Lord, our lives had changed dramatically in the seven years between Matt, our oldest, and Amber, our youngest, and I believed the changes had affected Amber. As I shared earlier in this chapter, Amber seemed unhappy and lonely and kept to herself around the house. During her crucial teen years, Ron and I were busy with our careers.

As I also wrote, I blamed Ron for Amber's wayward-ness. It's always easier to blame someone else, but in reality, I shared blame. I suffered guilt and held myself account-able. An amazing thing happens, though, when one stud-ies the Word of God. It brings wisdom and understanding. I repented of my failures and was able to let go of the past.

I was finished with self-condemnation. It was gone. In its place was God's grace.

And Jesus Whispered ~

My grace is sufficient, Kathi. It is enough— enough for every regret you face. Quit blaming yourself for your failures. I took away those failures when you became mine. I love you just as you are. Let my grace rain down upon you.

I had finally begun to understand amazing grace, so I released myself to God and threw down that heavy barrier, that invisible umbrella I'd been holding up, and felt His grace rain down on me. I was the little Kathi I remembered, who ran outside in the warm summer rains, who stood under a corner eave of the yellow house and washed her blonde hair in the soft rainwater flowing from the high roofs above. The little Kathi whose sundress was drenched, who had a smile on her face, and who laughed through the summer storm. And the refreshing grace now was sweeter than the warm rain had been then.

In his book, *Destined to Reign*, Joseph Prince writes, "Grace is not a theology. It is not a subject matter. It is not a doctrine. It is a person, and his name is Jesus. That's the reason the Lord wants you to receive the abundance of grace, for to have the abundance of grace is to have the abundance of Jesus."

I received the abundance of Jesus, and He was a welcomed whisper of grace, which in turn, strengthened my faith. Little did I realize how much I would rely on that faith in the days to come. That faith equipped me to help my parents, to talk things out with Ron, and to find ways to redemptively parent my adult children.

1. When might you have felt "broken" in your career, as I did? On two occasions in our marriage, Ron, our primary bread winner, was unemployed for an extended period of time. During those times, he, too, felt broken. Share how God sustained you in a time of brokenness.

2. As our parents age, our roles in life are sometimes altered or even reversed. How have you experienced those changes? If you could give one piece of advice regarding this role to someone who still has his or her parent[s], what would it be?

3. "Every happily married person I interviewed on my trip was grateful for his or her spouse, thanking God daily for one another," writes Fawn Weaver, in her book, Happy Wives Club: One Woman's Worldwide Search for the Secrets of a Great Marriage. It's not that thanking God makes the spouse a good person; but that thanking God helps you appreciate an already caring person. How might the simple step of thanking God daily for one's spouse make a huge difference? If you are married, list a number of things you could thank God for, regarding your spouse.

4. Dr. James Dobson, in his book Hide and Seek, writes, "Our task as parents is to begin very early to instruct our children on the true values of life." He then proceeds to list what he considers to be some of those key values of life, such as "integrity" and "trustworthiness." As you could infer in my earlier writing, after our children were grown, Ron and I had some regrets about the way we raised our children, and we discovered that many, if not most parents of grown children had similar regrets. If you are a parent of grown children, let's not focus on those regrets; instead, use your experiences to share what you now perceive to be the most important values parents should teach their

children. If you are not a parent, or if your children are still young, use your observations and knowledge to share those true values of life you recognize as most important. List five or more values you wish all parents would instill upon their children.

Whispers of Faith
Moving the Mountain with Mustard Seed Faith

Faith is the greatest of all the graces.
~JOSEPH PRINCE

I often write as I pray, so my journal was filled with the names of my precious family. Sometimes as I prayed, even though I'm not an artist, I sketched drawings of the sun or crosses or churches or angels or whatever might be connected with my prayer: "Angels protect," I had written beside one. As I had encouraged my English students to annotate their texts, I annotated insights from God's Word and applied the Word to myself. The Word encouraged and strengthened me. I read it, wrote next to it, and spoke it aloud.

> *"I will certainly be with you."* [31]

> *"Let us hold unswervingly to the hope we profess, for he who promised is faithful."* [32]

> *"Faith comes by hearing, and hearing by the Word of God."* [33]

I made notes of my prayer requests, and I made notes of praises. I prayed for "clean hands and a pure heart,"[34] for physical healing, for healing of our discouraged hearts, for increased faith, and I prayed the Psalms aloud and praised the LORD God.

It was through reading the Word of God that I recognized the enemy in this battle we were fighting for our daughter and her family. Paul defined the enemy in his instructions about putting on the armor of God:

> *"For our struggle is not against flesh and blood, but against the rulers, against the authorities, against the powers of this dark world and against the spiritual forces of evil in the heavenly realms."[35]*

I think I would have rather fought flesh and blood. Instead, the devil, himself, was our enemy. The day of facing this evil had come.

TAKING up THE SHIELD of FAITH

Through my written letters, I had been mailing the Word of God to Amber for months. Matt, Lynette, Kristen, and Josh were one with Ron and me—all united in prayer against the enemy. The Word told me that where two or more are gathered, Jesus is in the midst.[36] Jesus said that I could ask anything in his name, and he would do it,[37] that whatever I needed would be given to me.[38] The apostle John said that we can have confidence in approaching God: that if we ask anything according to his will, he hears us . . . and we have it.[39] Ron and I had been taught that when we pray, we should always ask for God's will in every matter, but there seemed to be a limitation on what we should ask. Oh, we could ask for anything, but we must always depend upon God's will, and that was the big mystery for us.

What was God's will? Was I asking according to His will?

I had accepted Jesus when I was young. I loved God, but I had spent much of my life in fear of God. My fear was not always a biblical fear that leads to wisdom, but a fear that didn't leave much room for God's grace. It didn't seem like my faith was truly the shield of faith I was reading about in Paul's letter to the Christians in Ephesus: "In addition to all this, take up *the shield of faith*, with which you can extinguish all the flaming arrows of the evil one . . . and the sword of the Spirit, which is the word of God."[40]

I examined the Sword of the Spirit (the Bible) to further examine my faith. I found that the markers and limitations I had previously put on God's grace and His will had changed—in fact, they had disappeared. Now I knew that if His Word told me a truth, I could pray that truth, knowing it was His will. So I did.

It was God's will that my daughter and her husband love and honor God. His Word told me so. I took up the shield of faith. Later, I developed a deeper insight of this shield. I realized that when I take up the shield, I am taking up His faithfulness. It is a piece of God's armor, given to me, enabling me to "stand [my] ground" in this "day of evil." Psalm 91, the great Psalm of Protection, told me that "his faithfulness [is my] shield and rampart" (91:4). His faithfulness "reaches to the skies,"[41] "meets with His love,[42] and "springs forth from the earth."[43] His faithfulness "endures forever,"[44] is "so great,"[45] and "goes before me"[46] in this battle. He not only goes before me, but he hems me in, behind and before.[47] He is ever faithful.

My faith was strengthened in this knowledge and continued to strengthen in every bit of *His* faithfulness I observed. I was called to "take up the shield,"[48] and when I did, my faith, if only the size of a mustard seed, through the authority of Jesus, had the power to move a mountain.[49]

Christmas came. We set a date for our family to gather at our house for our Christmas celebration. As usual, the cousins called and texted each other.

"When will you be here?" the children asked Amber's children, who in turn, questioned her. She had no answers. We waited and finally ate our bountiful Christmas dinner with five empty places around the table. It was disappointing, as usual, but I had learned to hold up and be strong for the others, especially for the grandchildren.

After dinner, Amber and the children arrived, without Jesse. Amber's eyes were red and swollen from crying. She was thin and looked worn.

We talked. We opened presents. We smiled. The cousins played. The love of family and the presence of the Holy Spirit permeated our home. The enemy would have wanted angry words spoken, strife, and discord. But our shields extinguished the flaming arrows of the evil one. And later, an amazing thing happened. We women were alone in the kitchen.

Lynette encouraged Amber. "You are a beautiful young woman, Amber. You can become anything you want. God wants you to be happy!"

Amber broke down and began to cry. Kristen, led by the Spirit of God, gathered us together. The four of us held each other and prayed. Amber was touched. We saw just a bit of the Amber we remembered. It seemed to us that when Amber went home that evening, she was a different person, but later we realized what we didn't know then. At those times, surrounded by strength, love, and support, she thought she wouldn't use drugs again. But in her home, surrounded by the demon of her addiction, she did.

The enemy doesn't give up easily.

After Christmas, I tried to maintain steady contact with Amber, but it was a one-sided effort. She never answered the phone. I had learned a way to get her to call me back: I would leave a message that I was coming over. She would usually call me right back so she could tell me not to come. One day, I left a message: "Dad and I are coming over."

And I didn't wait for her to return my call. It was another one of our unwanted visits to her home in Bronson, 20 miles away.

We went when the children were in school. We sat with Amber and Jesse at their table, and we all talked. Or perhaps I should say, Ron and I talked. We spoke of a hopeful future. We encouraged them. They were polite but avoided eye contact as much as possible. They were uneasy. We told them we'd like to pray for them. And we did. Our words were not rehearsed, but the Holy Spirit of God led us, and aside from our prayer, we rebuked the enemy in Amber and Jesse's home. Our children belonged to the Lord God Most High. They did not belong to the enemy, and we told him so.

We were at battle, but we were not alone. We had a leader. He was fighting for us. We were members of the army: "This is what the Lord says to you: 'Do not be afraid of discouraged because of this vast army [enemy]. For the battle is not yours, but God's . . . You will not have to fight this battle. Take up your positions; stand firm and see the deliverance the Lord will give you . . . Do not be afraid; do not be discouraged . . . the Lord will be with you."[50]

It was His battle. He would fight it for us. Our orders were to put on the armor and stand firm.

And Jesus Whispered ~

Stand firm, Kathi. Your enemy will be as nothing at all because I hold your right hand, I uphold you, I strengthen you, and I help you. I will never let you go. I go before you and I go behind you. I hem you in.

TRANSFORMING PARALYZING FEAR into FREEING FAITH

It was shortly after our visit to Amber and Jesse's house that we received the unwanted phone call – early in the night – between the normal Tuesday and the wretched Wednesday. That's when my wide-awake nightmare began.

You will not fear the terror of night, nor the arrow that flies by day, nor the pestilence that stalks in the darkness, nor the plague that destroys at midday. A thousand may fall at your side, ten thousand at your right hand, but it will not come near you (Psalm 91:5-7).

Day 1

That Wednesday morning was inwardly as dark to us as the long night had been, but daylight signaled us to get out of our uncomfortable bed and step into an even more uncomfortable world. The garish aura surrounded me and followed me from my bed, down the hall, and through the house. I was still hoping to waken, but like the nightmares of my childhood, I couldn't get away from the monster that was chasing me. The difference was now I knew the identity of the monster. It was the demon of meth.

We phoned our older children, Matt and Kristen, early that morning and told them the news. Their voices exposed their agony.

Jake called us again as soon as he had taken the kids to school. "The arraignment will be at 10:00 a.m. District Court."

What is an arraignment? Can we be there?

I don't remember eating or dressing or speaking that morning.

We walked into the courthouse, our faces swollen from crying appearing, I suppose, as though we were to face the judge ourselves. We recognized the deputy who stood guard at the entrance – a Christian friend from the community. He greeted us. News travels fast in our small town. His face divulged understanding and compassion.

"Place your purse on the belt please. Are you going upstairs? No cell phones allowed on the 2nd floor."

I don't know if we're going upstairs. "Where is the District Court?"

We did go upstairs, to the second floor. We did find the District Court room. It was empty. "Wait in the hall," someone said.

Jesse's dad Jake was there and Angela, Jesse's sister. We all hugged and cried as we had the year before, when Cyndi died. Now we tried to find comfort again, but I couldn't find it. I was numb.

Jake spoke of attorneys. He had already put a call in to a well-known attorney in town and was waiting his return call. The court would appoint an attorney for both Amber and for Jesse, and we could always hire a different attorney if we weren't satisfied with the one given us. *Us. This is not any more Amber's case than it is our own, my own. The fruit of my womb. My porcelain-complexioned, delicate-featured baby.*

We were gathered at the south end of the second floor, nearest the District Court room. A heavy door clanged open and shut at the opposite end of the hall, the echo rumbling toward us. Our heads turned toward the clamor. And then I saw my daughter, my beautiful little ivory faced baby, shuffling down the hall, beside her husband, shackled hand and foot, in faded orange and white stripes. Her now ashen and sunken face hung in shame and despair. It was more than I could bear. I twisted away and cried, "God, no." But God instantly turned me around to face my baby girl and to smile.

If my Lord could endure undeserved suffering, I can certainly endure this anguish. He is my strength. He understands.

"Don't touch them," the deputy demanded as they neared.

"We're here for you. We'll help you get through this," we all seemed to say in unison to our manacled loved ones.

Sometimes one is too weak to pray; sometimes no Scripture comes to mind. Just to speak His name helps. I whispered His name over and over. *Jesus. Jesus. Jesus.* And He whispered back.

And Jesus Whispered ~

In your day of trouble, just call to me, and I will answer. I am your Lord and I will help you.

The first of many days in court began.

The prosecutor presented the charges: Three felonies, each punishable by a 20-year prison sentence; three misdemeanors, including a high-court misdemeanor. Bond was set: $200,000 for Jesse; $100,000 for Amber.

The deputy led them away. Jesse and my baby girl, my precious child, out of the carpeted courtroom, scuffing down the tiled hall, back through the heavy secured door. The door slammed behind them, once again releasing metallic echoes down the hall. This time, I felt the ensuing invisible but painful lashes of those echoes, slapping me down, as my daughter and her husband were taken back to the jail.

Neither Ron nor I nor anyone in our family, had been arrested or had gone to court. How does one suddenly understand the criminal system? Arraignment? Bail?

Bond? And how does one have the strength to face the reality of three 20-year felonies and three misdemeanors, the possibility of our daughter facing 76 years in prison? It certainly wasn't by our strength. And now our strength was at its lowest. How could I ever rid my heart of the shock and distress of my daughter in an orange and white striped coverall, shackled hand and foot? *God, I can't bear this scene being replayed in my mind.* I asked the Lord to remove it from memory, and He did. Since that day, the vision has only come to my mind when I've discussed it or have written about it, which has imparted further evidence of His amazing grace, and has strengthened my faith in Him.

Child Protective Services (CPS) blended with the Department of Human Services (DHS). The caseworkers from both came to the arraignment and now awaited us in the hall, asking us to meet with them that afternoon. Ron and I wanted the children with us, in our home, safe and secure. We wanted to love them, hold them, comfort them, and assure them that everything would be all right. *Oh, God, why didn't you let the children come to us in the middle of the terrible night?* The meeting would include conference calls to Jesse and to Amber and would include deciding upon caretakers of the children. "Please bring names and birthdates of any of the children's relatives who want to be considered as caretakers of the children or who will want visiting time with the children," they informed us. Their words seemed strange. Others, outsiders, were telling me what was to be done with my grandchildren, *my* grandchildren. It was humbling, but I was quiet and listened.

Sometime between the morning arraignment and the afternoon meeting at DHS, Ron and I spoke to Matt and Kristen again. They insisted on getting Amber into a Rehab facility, should she be released from jail. Ron and I hadn't yet considered such an option. Rehab. Our minds were still foggy.

The afternoon meeting with DHS went well, I suppose, being unaware of how these meetings usually go. The caseworkers were impressed with us, all three grandparents present, showing love to each other. Jesse's sister-in-law, Dusty, was present. She and Jesse's brother wanted to take the children into their home where the children could live with their cousins, near their own schools. Our children, both Matt and Lynette and Kristen and Josh, desired to care for the children as well, but they both lived a distance away from the children's school system, much too far to drive daily. Certainly many family members loved and wanted to care for the children. We soon discovered it was an unusual situation.

"Oftentimes," a caseworker said, "no family members are present. We make the decisions without family input and the children are placed in foster homes. In this case, your case, the children have a loving family who want to care for them."

We wanted the children to live with us. I wanted to care for them, comfort them, and assure them everything would be all right. We soon learned that we would have to become foster parents to take our grandchildren into our home. *Foster parents? These are my grandchildren. I would give my life for them.* Background checks. Twelve hours of initial training. Continuing classes. Licensing. DHS would decide where and with whom the children would be placed. We had absolutely no control over the situation with our own grandchildren. I left the meeting in greater distress, longing to get the children settled in our home, but lacking any control to do so. DHS would schedule home visits in the next few days. Meanwhile, the children would remain with Jake.

This arrest was not what I had planned. For years, I had prayed for Amber and Jesse. Recognizing her depression and the turmoil in her life, I had begged her to get help, had begged her to make an appointment at a local behavior psychological clinic. I envisioned the scenario: She would receive counseling and get well. Now I wondered: *Why this arrest instead?*

Ron and I were in a limbo-like state, unable to focus. We walked around the house, not knowing what to do. Often, we held each other and dropped to our knees, crying and calling out to Jesus: *Help us.*

Sometime within the first 24 hours, I asked myself two simple questions: 1) *Is my faith real?* and 2) *Do I truly trust this God I've claimed to love?* I discovered answers that were also simple and clear: *Yes. He is my God, and I trust Him.*

Day 2

My nightmare continued throughout those first days after the arrest. I was numb, and God's grace was most difficult to see in the midst of my pain. Later, looking back, I knew that His grace was being extended to me in many little things. For instance, although I wanted the grandchildren with us and I yearned to hold them in my arms, God's grace allowed them to be with their Poppy (Jake) during those first days. Our grandchildren received love and care from Poppy and from their aunts and uncles living nearby. During those first days, I was able to face what was happening and gain strength to move forward; during those days, it was best that the grandchildren didn't see the uncertainty their Papa and I were facing and the distress I experienced when their mother phoned from jail. Yes, I was finding His grace in so many little things.

How does a mother cope with having her daughter in such anguish, calling and begging to get her out, crying that she can't bear another night in such a place, sobbing that she's cold and sick and miserable, pleading with me to sing to her? My heart didn't feel like singing, but I sang. I sang every lullaby and chorus I could remember in my broken state of being. When my mind went blank, I remembered the copy of a hymn I had received in the mail that day from my cousin, Lisa. It was folded inside a card. I rushed to the kitchen and opened the card. "Tell It to Jesus" was an old hymn I remembered from my childhood. I began to sing:

> Do the tears flow down your cheeks unbidden?
> Tell it to Jesus, Tell it to Jesus;
> Have you sins that to men's eyes are hidden?
> Tell it to Jesus alone.
> Tell it to Jesus, tell it to Jesus,
> He is a friend that's well known;
> You've no other such a friend or brother-
> Tell it to Jesus alone.
> Do you fear the gath'ring clouds of sorrow?
> Tell it to Jesus, Tell it to Jesus;
> Are you anxious what shall be tomorrow?
> Tell it to Jesus alone.

I sang to Amber until the automatic timer disconnected us. By then Amber had calmed, and I too was comforted by the reminder that I could tell Jesus all of my sorrows, that He was a friend like no other.

Not only was I reminded of my Savior's great love through song, but I was especially reminded when reading God's Word, the Bible. "The righteousness that is by faith says, 'The word is near you; it is in your mouth and in your heart; that is the word of faith.'"[51] I spoke the Word with my mouth, and I held it in my heart; thus in the weeks to follow, when I started blogging on my website, I centered my writing on the passage from Romans 10, in which Paul explained how Moses, in the Old Testament, had described righteousness that came from the law. Under the law, righteousness came from obedience, from doing (10:5). Then Jesus came! He brought the New Covenant. Now, we speak it with our mouths (10:9) and believe it with our hearts (10:10); thus, in this passage, Paul tells us that righteousness comes by faith in Jesus. He calls it *the Word of faith*. (10:8 NASB) This "faith comes from hearing the message . . . through the Word of Christ." (10:17) The more I read God's Word, the greater my faith became. It was near me—in my mouth and in my heart. And in those difficult days following my daughter's arrest, I spoke His Word, so thankful it was *near* me.

Although the judge had repeatedly referred to numerable, consecutive 20-year prison terms, my mind didn't comprehend or dwell on that word, *prison*. Instead, two full days passed before my mind processed the word *prison*. Two days of earnest prayers from our faithful Christian friends reached our loving God. Two days of gaining physical and mental strength allowed me to absorb the grace He offered—the grace I needed when I started to face what lie ahead for Amber and for all of us. Later, I realized this was continuing evidence of God's grace.

During those days, I heard someone speaking to the Father. I didn't recognize the voice, yet it was my own! My pleading prayer before the LORD God was unlike my former prayers. I spoke to God constantly—walking around the house, driving, walking the aisles of the grocery store. People sometimes stared. I wondered why. I didn't care. Prayer was the fuel that kept me going. Walking. Moving. Living. And that communion with God strengthened my faith.

> *Prayer is not asking. Prayer is putting oneself in the hands of God, at His disposition, and listening to His voice in the depth of our hearts.*
>
> -MOTHER TERESA

On that second day, I went into Amber and Jesse's house, intending to collect and bag the children's clothing. It was overwhelming. *Where do I start?* It was too much to sort in the clutter of their house. I gathered it all and took it home to launder, soon realizing it was too extensive a project for my home laundry. Ron and I took it all to the laundromat and the huge undertaking began. We shuddered at the idea of the greater task ahead – sorting, emptying, and cleaning their messy house. Too much to consider now. We would have to face it later.

My parents were both in a nursing home, and Ron's mother was in assisted living. I decided I would not visit any of them for a while, knowing I was quite transparent, and my face and demeanor would reveal the conflict within me. We wanted to protect them from the dreadful news of Amber's arrest, so I contacted both facilities and asked that their newspapers be kept from them. It was unlikely that either mother would hear the local television report, and if they did, perhaps by that time, I would have some better news to report rather than their granddaughter sitting in a jail cell. Certainly, my father wouldn't comprehend the news.

Late in the day, my Mama phoned. She was crying and distraught, having heard of Amber's arrest. I soon discovered that someone had decided to tell her. *Why did they tell her?* I thought. *What good could it possibly do? She's a helpless, elderly woman.* I tried to calm Mama before we hung up. My heart broke for her. Not only was *she* helpless, but because of my overwhelming tasks, I was helpless to go to the nursing home and attempt to calm her at this time. My initial reaction was one of anger and frustration. My old self would have called the person responsible and vented my anger on him or her. My new self knew that it wouldn't solve anything and would lead to regrets. I simply couldn't afford to add anger to my avalanche of emotions.

Instead, I contacted my sister and brother and asked that one of them go to the nursing home and comfort Mama. My brother went immediately and stayed with Mom until she slept later that night. The next days were difficult for her, too, but Larry spent much time with her. I learned a lesson from this unfortunate incident: We are all human and we sometimes disagree on decisions to be made, especially when we are hurting or in a stressful situation. And this was a stressful situation for us all. My sister and brother were faithful to Mama and Daddy during this difficult time when my daily visits ceased for about three weeks.

"I'm so worried about you, Kathi." I heard this statement repeatedly from family and friends.

"Please," I responded, "every time I come to your mind, pray instead."

I desperately needed their prayers. Other people, instead of expressing their worry, sometimes shared, and the sharing was painful. For instance, a friend told me about her nephew who also had been arrested on meth charges some years ago. He had been sentenced to prison and was still incarcerated. Considering prison tormented me. I was immediately nauseous. And I was terribly fearful.

In the prologue, I wrote about the prophet Elijah, who also was frightened. The concept of Elijah being fearful puzzled me at first and continued to bewilder me in further study. After all the demonstrations of God's power, Elijah was nonetheless so frightened by the threats of Jezebel that he ran more than 100 miles, where he collapsed under a broom tree. He then traveled another forty days and night to a cave at Mt. Horeb, where he hid. *Why,* I wondered, *would a prophet of God be so frightened? Why didn't he stand up to Jezebel and proclaim the Word of God to her, as he had proclaimed to so many others?* Whatever the reasons, I understood Elijah's fatigue and fears. I had been raised with fears. My family called it worry. My mother, father, aunts, and uncles had perfected worrying. It wasn't until later that I realized that worry although sometimes growing from godly concern, was typically nothing but fear. I too was adept at worrying. If my child was out of sight, and I sensed any possibility of danger, my mind could perceive the child dead and buried within seconds. The slightest fever brought visions of mortal illness and suffering. If there was a place to hide from my fears, I would certainly flee to it. Like Elijah.

I also learned about the Lord's unending patience with us and His tender love for us, His beloved children. Twice in the cave, the Lord questioned Elijah: "What are you doing here, Elijah?"[52] Certainly the Lord knew what was going on with Elijah, but His question allows us to know that the Lord did not call (or send) Elijah to this cave, as he had called him to other places in the past.[53] Although Elijah had not sought the Lord's direction in this matter of fleeing from Jezebel, our patient Lord did not chastise or punish him. Instead, the Lord simply and quietly spoke to Elijah, assuring him of His plan and directing him to his next calling.[54] Previously in Elijah's life, God had demonstrated His power with thunder and lightning and smoke and noise and fire.[55] But this time "the Lord was not in the wind . . . the earthquake, (or) the fire."[56] Instead, the Lord chose to speak to Elijah in a gentle whisper.[57] Elijah found the Lord in that gentle whisper heard *after* the tumult of the wind, earthquake, and fire, and he pulled his cloak over his face,[58] most likely as a sign of humility and respect. In evident trust and faith, Elijah obeyed the Lord and went where the Lord sent him. Now I, too, can hear the gentle whisper of the Lord, and give all my worries and cares to Him because He cares for me.[59] "Faith comes from hearing" the wonderful message, the good news, the Word of Christ.[60] As I listen and hear the message, my paralyzing fear can be turned into freeing faith.

When my friend shared news of her nephew's imprisonment, and fear invaded my heart and mind, I went to the Word of God. I wrote about it in my journal:

Even as I write this, the phone interrupts. Troubles surface in my mind. Fear creeps through my body. Anxiety pervades my heart. I speak words of doubt. Then I review today's devotion from *Pursuit of His Presence*. Gloria Copeland wrote, "Did you know that the devil can't do anything to you if you won't give him any place? That's right. If you won't speak words of doubt and unbelief, but instead speak Words of faith, he can't sustain his attack . . . keep talking faith." The word is near me; that word of faith is in my mouth and in my heart. These days, I must constantly remember to keep talking faith.

"Set a guard over my mouth, O Lord; keep watch over the door of my lips." [61]

He whispers to me about speaking faith rather than words of doubt and fear.

And Jesus Whispered ~

Guard your heart, Kathi, for it is the wellspring of your life. Fill this wellspring with nothing but my words. Don't let my words out of your sight; keep them in your heart; they are life to you and health to your body. Remember, guard your heart. Guard your mouth, as well. Speak my word. Speak truth. Speak grace. Speak faith. And know my mercy.

Jesus-Whispers for You

1. In this chapter I shared several references to God's faithfulness, most of which are from the Psalms, yet the entire Bible is full of evidence of God's faithfulness. How do the following verses speak about God's faithfulness?

1 Thessalonians 5:24

2 Timothy 2:13 and Romans 3:3

Hebrews 10:23

2. In this chapter, I wrote, "My nightmare continued throughout those first days . . . Later, looking back, I knew that His grace was being extended to me in many little ways." Think back on your life and ask God to bring to mind times when you have recognized His faithfulness. List them below. Consider keeping a notebook or journal in which you record these times. How might these notations encourage you in your relationship with Him, especially in times of trial?

3. I wrote, "How does a mother cope with having her daughter in such anguish? . . . My heart didn't feel like singing, but I sang!" Many of you have suffered along with one who is in anguish, sick, or dying—perhaps your child, your spouse, or your parent—yet somehow you sang when you didn't feel like it. How was that possible?

4. Why do some people, even believers sometimes speak doom and gloom? How do you deal with discouraging comments in a Christ-like manner?

5. Has fear invaded your heart and mind at times? Where have you fled out of fear? Where has your mind taken you due to fear? Consider 2 Timothy 1:7: "For God has not given us a spirit of fear and timidity, but of power, love, and self-discipline (a sound mind)" (NLT). If God has not given us a spirit of fear, who has? Read Psalm 3:1-3; Psalm 26:11-12; and Psalm 32:7. Then write a prayer of thanksgiving for the deliverance the Lord offers from those things which you fear.

chapter four

WHISPERS OF MERCY
Recognizing God's Mercy in Our Midst

God's mercy is ultimate comfort, but it is also a call to a brand-new way of living. God's mercy really does change everything forever, for all upon whom this mercy is bestowed
~PAUL DAVID TRIPP

In his "Notes on Romans," Dr. Thomas L. Constable quotes Thomas Griffith: "Men fit themselves for hell; but it is God [who] fits men for heaven." For many years, although a believer, I had seen myself as more fit for hell than for heaven. I was filled with guilt and condemnation. That wrong believing began to change, as The Holy Spirit worked a wonder in my broken heart. Though I could do nothing to alter my situation or that of my daughter, God enlightened the eyes of my heart to "the riches of his glorious inheritance" in me.[62] God began to display the "riches of his glory"[63] to me, or rather, I began to see them, as I listened to His whispers.

And Jesus Whispered ~

I call you "mine." I call you "my loved one."
You are an object of my mercy.

I finally saw myself as His "loved one," an "object of His mercy"! [64]

TRUSTING in HIS FAVOR

> *For they did not gain possession of the land by their own sword, Nor did their own arm save them; But it was Your right hand, Your arm, and the light of Your countenance, Because You favored them* (Psalm 44:3 NKJV).

Although I had always believed "God made him [Jesus] who had no sin to be sin for us, so that in him we might become the righteousness of God,"[65] I assumed, nonetheless, that my holiness was produced by my efforts and therefore must be maintained by my efforts. My head knew I was saved by grace, not of my own works,[66] yet I had always felt that God would punish me for any wrong I might do. It was wrong believing for sure.

I had known Jesus as Savior since I was ten years old, but now as I totally trusted Him in my helplessness, I realized that He loved me with an unfailing love. He was my single comfort at the time. I trusted that He loved Amber, Jesse, and the children. This arrest was not what I wanted, and now I knew that it was not what Jesus wanted either. I trusted that He would change all this bad into good. Why? Because I had His favor.

Favor. It was a new concept to me yet suddenly as familiar as though I had always fully recognized it. Although verses about God's favor were clear in the Bible, I had never truly considered them. Many people were praying for me; someone must have been praying that I would understand the tremendous love and favor of the Father because, at this worst point in my life, I did!

> *For surely, O Lord, you bless the righteous; you surround them with your favor as with a shield (Psalm 5:12).*

> *[Do not] receive God's grace in vain. For he says, "In the time of my favor I heard you, and in the day of salvation I helped you." I tell you, now is the time of God's favor, now is the day of salvation (2 Corinthians 6:1-3).*

Favor. Undeserved. Unmerited. But it was mine: the Favor of the Father. And it was all because of Jesus. It was the New Covenant of His body, given for me, and of His blood, shed for me.[67] I had spent most of my adult life in condemnation and guilt—never feeling good enough for

God's grace. But now, when I needed it the most, I realized, recognized, and received His amazing grace and His unfailing love for me and for my family. It was an awesome understanding that filled my broken heart. Almighty God had given me His favor.

> *Faith is seeing light with your heart when all*
> *your eyes see is darkness.*
> *~Barbara Johnson*

"In the beginning . . . God saw that the light was good, and he separated the light from the darkness . . . And there was evening, and there was morning—the first day."[68] God created light on that first day. Light, separated from the darkness. Incarnate Jesus is the Light of the World. This Light, Jesus Christ, became righteousness for us. Because of Jesus, I am righteous. And because I am righteous, I have received His favor.

And Jesus Whispered ~

> *I bless you, Kathi because you are righteous in*
> *Christ Jesus. I have surrounded you with my*
> *favor as a shield.*

In the book of John, we read about Jesus healing the man who had been blind from birth: "His disciples asked him, "Rabbi, who sinned, this man or his parents, that he was born blind?" (John 9:2).

Who sinned? I wondered. *Why has this terrible thing happening to us? Was it Amber's sin? Ron's? Mine?* His Word answered: "'Neither this man nor his parents sinned,' said Jesus, 'but this happened so that the work of God might be displayed in him'" (John 9:3). The Light of the World brought grace to the blind man, and that same grace now rained down upon me, flooding me with His love and with an understanding of His favor. I soaked it in, His grace and His favor. And I had done nothing to deserve it. It was all because He loved me.

Jesus still is the Light of the World, and I soon found that His light was to shine in not only my life, but in Amber's life, as well.

Two days after the arrest, Amber phoned crying. She was cold in her cell and felt ill much of the time. Her skin was dry and chapped. No lotion was available. No shampoo was given for her hair. Of course my heart ached as any mother's heart would, thinking of my daughter, who I knew was thin and weak and sickly, cold in her cell at night. I called the office of the jail and was told that I could put money in Amber's account. This account could fund supplies, such as long johns to be worn under the striped coveralls. Those supplies could be ordered on Thursday and delivered the following Monday. I counted the cold nights until Monday. It was four too many. I drove to the jail, about ten miles from our home, located the side entrance near the office, and asked to speak to the Captain (Warden). They paged him. He came to the window near me. I asked if I could possibly bring Amber some warm long johns, that she was already sick and I didn't want her to be cold until Monday. I saw a hardened face soften with compassion. "How quickly can you get the long johns back here?" he asked, adding, "They'll need to be in the original store packaging."

"Within a half an hour," I responded. God's favor surrounded me. My daughter was warm that night. Now, I was beginning to comprehend not only God's favor but also His marvelous mercy to us in this time of pain. And He had shown me a specific way to love my daughter.

Late in the day, during one of those agonizing phone calls with Amber in jail I said, "Amber, it's just you and God now." I felt helpless when I said it, yet relieved in knowing that she was with God alone. He loved her even more than I did, and I realized that now.

Day 3

Late on Friday, I received another collect call from Amber. She was crying, panic-stricken, and distraught. I told her I would call the jail and ask the nurse to see her. She begged me not to call, saying that they would put her in solitary confinement and she couldn't bear it. After the call, I phoned the jail chaplain, Dave Brown. "Please go visit Amber," I pled.

"Do you think she might be suicidal?" he asked.

I had never considered such a thing.

"I don't know," I confessed.

Shortly, Chaplain Dave called me back. "I reached one of my female volunteers," he said. "We'll go in and visit Amber this evening."

Chaplain Dave was a layman at the church where Cyndi's funeral was held, and he served as the jail chaplain through Forgotten Man Ministries. Years before, he had fished with Jake and the boys. He had watched Jesse as a little boy sitting on a stump at the edge of the lake, casting out his line; he had followed Jesse's baseball career through high school; he had ministered to Jake in his recent grief; and now he oversaw the Christian ministry at the jail where Jesse and Amber were being held. I detected a few of many puzzle pieces, meticulously assembled by the Lord God, which now revealed glimpses of the finished picture. It was further evidence to me of God's wonderful mercy.

Later that evening, I found a message on my phone: "Kathi, this is Chaplain Dave. We went in to visit Amber this evening. She rededicated her life to Jesus Christ. I think she's doing well. There are other ladies there to encourage her and build her up in the faith."

My relief was palpable—relief in Amber's physical and mental conditions—and relief that she had rededicated herself to the Lord. In my state of distress, I didn't recognize the depth of this blessing. It took a while to realize that it was all because of God's favor.

Matt and Kristen had researched and contacted rehab and recovery facilities for their sister, and they had decided upon Kalamazoo Gospel Mission in Kalamazoo, Michigan. They were adamant that upon Amber's release on bail, she must immediately go into a recovery program. We trusted their judgment and agreed with them. Our first jail visitation with Amber was scheduled for late Saturday morning.

Day 4

Matt and Kristen arrived at our house Saturday morning to discuss our plan of action in visiting Amber. Two visitors were allowed, but we were hoping all four of us would be able to see her, perhaps two at a time. We had never visited anyone in jail, so we didn't know protocol. Since Ron and I had both been able to speak to Amber on the phone throughout the last few days, we decided that Kristen and Matt would meet with her first. Ron and I would wait if only two visitors were allowed. The plan was that Kristen would first talk to Amber. Kristen had a list of questions prepared. Amber's answers would reveal her state of mind and her spiritual condition. Then Matt would tell Amber that we had arranged for her to go to a recovery program at the Kalamazoo Gospel Mission. We expected her to resent and resist the decision, but we agreed to be firm and offer her no choice in the matter. If time permitted, Ron and I would talk to her.

We drove to the jail, which I had passed many times in my life on my way elsewhere, to the grocery store or to school. Today, it was my destination. Shortly before 11 a.m., we parked and walked toward the visitors' entrance. I encouraged the others to stay strong in front of Amber. I was determined to hold up during our visit, but I fully expected to break down when we left. We entered the east door where about a dozen people had already gathered to visit their family members. I looked at their sad faces. Although we lived in a small town, I didn't recognize anyone, but there was a bond among us; we were all broken, hurting people. We signed in, presented driver's licenses, and filled out forms. We waited. At 11 a.m., the officer unlocked and opened a steel door. About twenty people filed out, including a number of children. One visitation was over and another was about to begin. The officer allowed all four of us to enter. We followed the other visitors who seemed to know the routine.

We entered a narrow, long room filled with cubicles, each with an outdated phone attached to the dividing walls, a bench bolted to the floor, and a small wall of glass, designed to separate the visitor from the inmate. The steel door closed loudly behind us. The other visitors quickly and habitually took places at the various cubicles, obviously familiar with the practice. We followed their lead, Kristen and Matt sitting on the bench, nearest the phone. The female inmates filed in through a door on their side of the glass—all looking strikingly similar in their orange and white striped coveralls, their disheveled hair, and their lonely eyes, All looking much like my Amber. They took their places across the glass from their family visitors and began their conversations over their phones.

Where is my daughter? Did they forget to inform her she has visitors? Are they refusing to allow her visitors for some reason?

But there she was, the last in line looking not at all as I expected.

Amber entered the room with a Bible under her arm and a smile on her face. Her eyes lit up when she saw us all. I stared in awe as she and Kristen maneuvered to get their phones connected. Amber's once pallid face now glowed, her sunken cheeks filled, her eyes sparkled, her lips were smooth and rosy, and her hair was clean and shiny. Her head was raised. She made eye contact with us, unlike in the past, when she had hung her head and avoided looking at us. I stared, speechless and baffled at observing the first physical miracle of my life.

Kristen asked her the questions she had planned. With each response, we all became more excited. We soon realized the phone was unnecessary, as we all could hear each other through the glass. Matt told her of our plans to take her to the Kalamazoo Gospel Mission as soon as we could get her released. "Oh, good," she replied. She asked our forgiveness for the hurt she had caused us; she spoke of redemption and how thankful she was that her days of lies and deceit were over. Our 30-minute visit became 30 minutes of praise and worship together! Instead of falling to my knees in agony, as I had expected to, when I left the building, I raised my hands in praise and thanksgiving to my Lord God. My daughter was redeemed. We had witnessed a miracle of God.

And Jesus Whispered ~

I have great plans for you and yours, Kathi, and none of those plans are for harm. They are all plans for a good and bright future.

My daughter now had a future. We all had a bright future. It was all because of God's amazing grace, love, and mercy.

Leave the broken, irreversible past in God's hands, and step out into the invincible future with Him.
~Oswald Chambers

Day 5

Another transforming miracle of God occurred on Sunday. Chaplain Dave later shared the story. As he sat in church that morning, it was as though a neon light flashed in front of him, catching his attention: *Jesse. Jesse. Jesse.* He immediately left the service, drove to the jail, and called Jesse out of his cell.

Jesse later shared his story. When not forced to go to meals or to shower, he had been sleeping his time away in his jail cell, partly due to withdrawal of the drug and largely due to depression. He didn't know if Amber was still in jail, if or when he would ever again see her or his children, or what his future held. It was much easier to sleep than to think about it. When Jesse was summoned out of his cell, the Light of the World—the Light I wrote about earlier, which had brought grace to the blind man, grace to me, and grace to Amber—suddenly filled the darkness in Jesse's life. Everything in Jesse's life was exposed by the Light and made visible to him. God's Word penetrated Jesse's heart at that moment, saying, "Wake up, O sleeper, rise from the dead, and Christ will shine on you."[69] He sat across a table from Chaplain Dave.

"Jesse, are you ready to receive Jesus Christ as your Savior?"

"Yes, I am," he replied.

> *He keeps his promises and does not want anyone to be lost. He wants each of us to come to repentance* (2 Peter 3:9).

Isn't God's favor awesome?

Tending to Necessities

By this fifth day, I began to focus on what lie ahead. It was quite overwhelming, so I tried to take one step at a time. My first priority was the children. Ron and I desperately wanted them with us. DHS would be coming to inspect the house within a few days, and I wanted to be ready. People assured us that DHS would place the children with us, but I wasn't certain. I wanted everything perfect to increase our chances. On Sunday afternoon my cousin, Sherri and my friend, Debbie came to the house to help me clean and arrange. Bless their hearts! They cleaned and sorted and organized. After this boost, I worked to get the children's potential bedrooms ready. Not only did I want the house perfect for the DHS home visit, but I wanted the house ready for our three grandchildren, a home they could call their own for as long as they would live with us. Our two extra (guest) bedrooms, were now redecorated for the three grandchildren. Kaylee's room was bright with pinks and chenille on the French Provincial bed her mommy had once slept in. The matching dresser, covered with pictures of her mommy and daddy, already held new clothes I had purchased for her. A large photo of her mommy at Kaylee's age, like her twin, was pinned to her bulletin board. The boys' room held double beds, both covered in brown and green comforters dotted with fireflies and frogs. A matching lamp sat on one of their dressers, and each dresser had pictures of them with their mom and dad. Their mom and dad's wedding picture sat on a shelf. Jacob's favorite posters were pinned to the wall by his bed, while Ben's outgrown but highly treasured t-shirts were pinned to his wall. The children's rooms provided subtle, reassuring reminders that their family was still intact, although separated for a time.

Day 6

On Monday, Amber phoned collect from the jail and shared a passage of Scripture with me. The verses described her former life: dark, ignorant, insensitive, and sensual, contrasted with her new life: created to be like God, righteous and holy, putting off falsehood, speaking truthfully, being wholesome and an imitator of God.

> So I tell you this, and insist on it in the Lord, that you must no longer live as the Gentiles do, in the futility of their thinking. They are darkened in their understanding and separated from the life of God because of the ignorance that is in them due to the hardening of their hearts. Having lost all sensitivity, they have given themselves over to sensuality so as to indulge in every kind of impurity, and they are full of greed. That, however, is not the way of life you learned when you heard about Christ and were taught in him in accordance with the truth that is in Jesus. You were taught, with regard to your former way of life, to put off your old self, which is being corrupted by its deceitful desires; to be made new in the attitude of your minds; and to put on the new self, created to be like God in true righteousness and holiness. Therefore each of you must put off falsehood and speak truthfully to your neighbor, for we are all members of one body. "In your anger do not sin": Do not let the sun go down while you are still angry, and do not give the devil a foothold. Anyone who has been stealing must steal

no longer, but must work, doing something useful with their own hands, that they may have something to share with those in need. Do not let any unwholesome talk come out of your mouths, but only what is helpful for building others up according to their needs, that it may benefit those who listen. And do not grieve the Holy Spirit of God, with whom you were sealed for the day of redemption. Get rid of all bitterness, rage and anger, brawling and slander, along with every form of malice. Be kind and compassionate to one another, forgiving each other, just as in Christ God forgave you. Follow God's example, therefore, as dearly loved children and walk in the way of love, just as Christ loved us and gave himself up for us as a fragrant offering and sacrifice to God.[70]

I dated and marked the passage in my Bible. And I rejoiced. *This is my daughter, Amber, sharing Scripture of her changed life in Christ. Truly our God is a God of miracles.*

My cousin, Sherri, arranged for a prayer meeting at her house that evening. Our closest friends were there. It was a special time of prayer. Ron and I could sense their love and concern, but we also sensed a foreboding impression of gloom. At the time, it seemed that no one stood with us in believing that God would spare Amber from a prison sentence. I looked at their long, saddened faces and felt alone in my faith. *Was I was blinded by my hope? Was I not seeing things clearly? Was my hope in vain? Was Amber doomed to prison? Certainly others with similar charges had made agreements with the courts or had some charges reduced.*

And Jesus Whispered ~

I love you with an unfailing love, Kathi. Though your world is shaken, my love for you is not. I am going before you. I will break down the gates of bronze and cut through the bars of iron.

Even in our weakened conditions, God had given Ron and me an understanding of His unfailing love for us and evidence of His amazing grace toward us, an unexplainable phenomena that we knew in the depths of our souls. This strengthened our faith and stretched it to heights it had never touched before. Perhaps that faith which we had increasingly experienced was not known to our closest friends in those moments. Perhaps they didn't need it during those days, as we did. Yet God used our closest friends and others to minister to our great physical, emotional, and spiritual needs. They were our allies and they reminded us of their love for us and our family through their concern shown us in phone calls, cards and notes, email messages, hugs, and simply being good listeners when we needed them.

In the book of Acts, Luke wrote of accompanying the Apostle Paul to Rome. Paul had suffered imprisonment and shipwreck, and was undoubtedly tired and worn. In Rome, friends in Christ heard of Luke's and Paul's arrival and traveled to meet them. "At the sight of these men Paul thanked God and was encouraged" (Acts 28:15). This is how Ron and I felt when we saw our friends and family, those who were supporting us and praying for us. We thanked God and were encouraged by their sight.

When Elijah was hiding in the cave, frightened and discouraged, the Lord helped him by reminding him that he was not alone in his efforts, that "seven thousand in Israel"[71] were faithful to God. Elijah's ordeal reminded me that Ron and I were not alone in our journey. Our friends who were our fellow believers, "members of one another,"[72] the "body of Christ,"[73] were surrounding us and lifting us up to God the Father. We would carry this lesson from Elijah's experience and one day use it to surround others when they were weak.

And Jesus Whispered ~

You are not alone, Kathi. Others are with you, ministering to you in my name. I hear their prayers, and I take those prayers to the Father.

Ron's employer graciously gave him time off work for the court arraignment, meetings, and hearings. My dean at the college did the same. I had a minimal teaching schedule that semester, so instead of Ron, I handled many of the responsibilities we now faced. The prayers of our faithful family and friends gave us strength to move forward. It was not a day-to-day process, nor was it an hour-to-hour process; it was moment-by-moment. Fears came. I felt weak. I constantly reminded myself that prayers for me were going before Lord. *Aunt Carolyn is praying for me. Sue is praying for me.* I told myself that it would be insulting to God not to trust Him. The prayers covered me, moment by moment. I forced myself not to dwell on my fears. I prayed Scripture and spoke 2 Timothy 1:7 repeatedly: "God did not give me the spirit of fear, but He gave me a spirit of power and of love, and of a sound mind" (NKJV paraphrased).

Day 7

I drove an hour to the Kalamazoo Gospel Mission, the facility Kristen and Matt had chosen for Amber's Rehab and Recovery. It was not a pleasant visit. I had hoped for an attractive facility, with a lodge-like atmosphere, an outdoor sitting area with trees and flowers. A place of safety and refuge. Instead I drove from an attractive downtown to a parking lot on the edge of town. A timeworn, brick, two-story building hugged broken sidewalks and barren patches of land, filled the other three quarters of the block.

My heart sank. This was the Mission. The local bus station was nearby and ragged railroad tracks crossed the adjoining streets. I found it difficult to find entry to the building, but once inside people directed me through a gaudy, dark blue-painted hallway, encased with outdated painted lockers, to the office of Maureen. She served as one of the directors. A few children played in what looked like a former church sanctuary. Young women, apparently their mothers, sat in dark plastic chairs to the side, waiting. For what, I don't know. One of the children wrapped her arms around my legs and hugged me. A young couple, prematurely aged by experience, stood outside Maureen's office. He was tattooed and held a baby. She was bloated from pregnancy and childbirth. Both looked terribly unhappy. They also waited.

I couldn't imagine my beautiful Amber in this place. But maybe the people were the beauty here. Maureen caught my eye. She attended church with Kristen and had worked at the Kalamazoo Gospel Mission for years. Now she welcomed me and took me on a tour of the facilities. We went through a back door from her office leading to the ugly, dark, blue-painted hallway again and then into a slightly brighter hallway. She opened a door. "Amber will spend the first few nights here," she said. "The door will be ajar, so we can come in throughout the night to check her." She knew Amber's name and spoke it with kindness. The small room held two barrack-style bunks. "She'll share it with two to three other ladies."

I commented that the room and bunks would probably appeal to Amber after 10-12 days in jail. She then took me into another wing of the building to a bit larger room where Amber would go next, then past the dining room where she would eat her meals, and finally, into yet another wing where her classrooms would be. By the time we returned to Maureen's office, I broke into tears. "Do you know of any nicer places we could take Amber?" I asked. She smiled and shook her head. *No.*

"We hope to bring her on Thursday or Friday," I said. "If the judge will release her."

I drove to the mall to shop for clothing for the kids. I was crying so hard in the department store that a stranger asked if she could do something to help me.

"No."

I don't remember if I bought anything that day or not. I remember that as I headed for home and was ready to enter the highway, I pulled over to the side knowing I wasn't fit to drive in this condition. Sobbing, I phoned my daughter, Kristen. She was taken aback to hear me in this state of despair. She encouraged me, reminding me to trust God and to know He wanted to bless Amber and us. I realized three things: One, that each of us—Ron, Kristen, Matt, and me each traveled this journey differently and that was okay; two, that I could be refreshed by the encouragement of others, even when they didn't fully understand; and three, that I truly could trust God.

And Jesus Whispered ~

I will never leave you, Kathi, nor forsake you. I will never leave Amber, nor forsake her. I

am your God. You are my child. I have cho-
sen you, Kathi, and not rejected you. So do
not fear, for I am with you. I will strengthen
you and will uphold you.

Day 8

A hearing was set for Thursday. We needed to be ready, but we had no idea what to expect. Ron and I called Amber's court-appointed attorney and asked to meet with him. To our knowledge, he had not yet met with Amber.

The attorney was intimidating, to say the least. We didn't understand his legal jargon. He was firm, appeared arrogant, and within minutes, I assumed we would leave his office to hire a different attorney. But by the time we left his office we realized that he was the perfect attorney for us. Feisty and determined, he knew exactly how to help Amber. I saw the strengths in his firmness. I was beginning to learn that God plans situations so much better than I do.

Every day was difficult for Amber in jail. She sat in her cell, apparently unaware of the steps we were taking to get her released. Her occasional collect phone calls revealed frustration but, thank God, no longer the despair of the previous week. She mentioned her bed at our house. She asked *if* she was released to be able to spend one night in the comfort of her childhood bed, the one I was preparing for Kaylee at home. It was a small request, one we wanted to grant, but both Kristen and Matt believed we should take her directly from the jail to the recovery facility. Their research into rehab suggested this plan. Kristen planned to be at the hearing on Thursday to assure it would happen.

DHS made their home visit. How strange and invasive it felt to have someone inspect my home to see if it met specifications for caring for my grandchildren. If the children were placed with us, Ron and I would have to become their foster parents and take classes to learn to care for them. I had raised three children, had cared for my nine grandchildren, and would have given my life for any one of them. But DHS was in control. It was humiliating, but I humbled myself.

Finally, we needed to contact a bondsman. We would have to pay a bondsman ten percent of the bail, which then became his unreturnable fee. $10,000 was an immense amount of money for us. Amber's attorney hoped to get her bail reduced to $50,000, which would mean a $5,000 fee to the bondsman. We were hoping for that reduction in bail, but just in case, we took $10,000 out of our meager retirement savings. If the judge allowed, we would use it to get our daughter released from jail the next day.

We were worn, weary, financially-concerned, and troubled. I prayed, back and forth, from my heart to the heart of Jesus. I knew He was listening because I often heard Him whisper back.

And Jesus Whispered ~

I am with you. I am mighty to save. I take great delight in you, Kathi. I rejoice over you with singing. Let my love quiet you today.

I wrote about His faithful love:

> Simple sounds have turned to cacophony.
> Music has turned to dissonance.
> *The Lord your God will quiet you with his love.*

> As much as she tries to rid herself of the bondage, the grief remains.
> *The Lord your God will quiet you with his love.*

> Waves are crashing.
> She can't hold her head above water.
> *The Lord your God will quiet you with his love.*

> She feels stifled. She can't breathe.
> *The Lord your God will quiet you with his love.*

She sees nothing but pain ahead—pain and disappointment.
The Lord your God will quiet you with his love.

She can't take another day.
She is confused, frustrated, angry, overwhelmed.
The Lord your God will quiet you with his love.

She wants to give up the fight.
It's not worth it any more.
The Lord your God will quiet you with his love.

Tasting His Goodness

> *The angel of the LORD encamps around those who fear him, and he delivers them. Taste and see that the LORD is good; blessed is the man who takes refuge in him (Psalm 34: 7, 8).*

Day 9

Thursday was a whirlwind. A good whirlwind. We didn't know what to expect at this hearing, both because of our ignorance of legal affairs and our understanding that Amber's future rested in the judge's hands. No one, not even the attorneys, knew what the judge would decide at this first hearing. We arrived early. Amber was to meet with her attorney. Jesse was to meet with his. Jake had hired an out-of-town attorney for Jesse, paying a $7,000 deposit for services. We were hoping the attorneys would work wonders. Perhaps we would see Amber and Jesse before the hearing. Perhaps their attorneys would be available to talk to us. We met Jake in the hall outside the courtroom. Ron waited there while I stepped into the nearby south stairwell.

This day was the first of many I would spend in that stairwell. Looking out the south window. Praying. Singing. Reading aloud God's promises from the Bible. I had asked Ron to let me know if Amber came down the hall, if the attorney would talk to us, or when it was time for us to enter the courtroom. And so I stood in the stairwell and communed with the Lord while I waited. Others came and gathered with Ron and Jake in the hall above me—family and friends of ours and of Jake's. Their presence was comforting. They were our allies. They didn't judge us or Amber and Jesse. They backed us up and supported us at our lowest point.

Ron came to the stairwell and called me up to the hallway. "Amber and Jesse are coming down the hall." I had prepared myself this time. I knew to expect the ugly orange and white stripes and the cuffs. But I hadn't prepared myself for the pain I observed in the faces of our allies who were present. My heart ached once again. For them. For Amber. For me. This group of people, our allies, who cared so much for Amber and for Jesse, shared common emotions: tenderness toward our broken couple and the painful sting of sin and lawlessness.

We followed our young couple into the courtroom, found seats, and waited quietly. The judge entered the courtroom. Formalities began, again foreign to us, but we were beginning to learn the lingo. The prosecutor spoke. Others at his table supported him. They felt like our enemies, yet I knew our enemy was much greater than this man and his assistant. Our enemy was the devil and his demonic underlings. We were at the mercy of the court, a typical but nonetheless terrifying step in the progression resulting from breaking the law and facing the consequences. But the arms of the just God were around me. He had said, "I will have mercy on whom I have mercy, and I will have compassion on whom I have compassion."[74] He enveloped me in His mercy and compassion.

Both attorneys spoke. Amber's attorney assured the judge that her family had arranged for her to enter a rehab and recovery program. The judge then actually encouraged Jesse's attorney to find a similar program for Jesse. The judge told Amber and Jesse how fortunate they were to have such family love and support. I regarded the judge as a man of wisdom. Relief flooded me when he announced that both Amber and Jesse could be released on bond that day. Then the judge made an unexpected statement. Instead of lowering their bail to $50,000 as we had hoped, he lowered their bail to $20,000, an amount that did not require a bondsman but could be paid by family in the amount of ten percent. Just $2,000. And only ten percent of the $2000 would be kept by the court. Later, after the sentencing, $1,800 would be returned to us. We were all shocked by this decision. Now, I was beginning to recognize the mercy of God through the mercy of the judge. And it was the first evidence of God's mercy on that Thursday.

Suddenly, Amber and Jesse were taken from the courtroom, while our group rejoiced in the judge's decision to release them and to reduce bond. *What was to be done now?* I wondered. We hurried to the jail to pay the bail money. During this time, DHS met with us about a plan for the children to be able to see their parents. Their Aunt Dusty was picking them up from school in Bronson. DHS asked her to bring the children to the DHS office in Coldwater, where they could visit their mother and father for a short time upon release. Again, we were pleasantly surprised in a legal decision made that day. DHS would allow the children to see their parents.

We paid Amber's bail; Jake paid Jesse's; and they were both released. We took them to the DHS office where they met with their children. It was a short visit and lacked privacy, but nonetheless became a special time for the shattered family of five. Arrangements were made for the children to then spend the night with their Aunt Kristen, whom DHS had approved. They couldn't be with us since Amber was coming home with us, nor could they be with Jake since Jesse would be with him. It all happened quickly. Kristen took the children home with her, and we took Amber home with us to her childhood home, a place of comfort and refuge for her. Due to the unexpected, hurried events of the day and the approaching evening, Amber's desire to spend one night in the comfort of her childhood bed would be granted. Our precious little porcelain-faced daughter was fragmented but because she was in the arms of our loving, merciful God, she would be healed.

Jake and Jesse came for supper. Our fellowship was sweet, unlike any we'd ever had. It was a night of rejoicing. Neither Ron nor I recognized Jesse; he was a new man. He used words like *glorious*. He and Amber spoke of their new life together and their future hopes. For the first time in ten days, I knew joy. And it was all because of Jesus and His mercy.

And Jesus Whispered ~

I make all things new! The old is gone. Your children have been made new in their attitudes. They've been made righteous and holy.

Day 10

We discovered we had made the right decision in allowing Amber to spend one night at our home. Thursday night had been dark, dreary, cold, and not a good evening to have taken her to the lonely-feeling surroundings of Kalamazoo Gospel Mission. Friday's weather wasn't much better, but it had to be done. Jake and Jesse had spent the night. They left early in the morning after Jesse and Amber held each other and said their goodbyes, not knowing when they would see each other again or what their futures held. Each faced up to 76 years in prison. They were thankful to have had time together after ten days apart. Soon, Ron and I took Amber to Kalamazoo.

I had packed bedding and toiletries for Amber, and we stopped along the way to purchase more things she might need. Arriving at Kalamazoo Gospel Mission, we were met by Maureen. We stayed a short time, somewhat anxious to leave Amber there as though each moment was one moment closer to her recovery. Amber responded well to being there. Relieved, we hugged our darling daughter, left her in the strange new place, and drove to Kristen's house about 30 minutes away to pick up Jacob, Ben, and Kaylee for the weekend, a visit arranged by DHS.

Barely an hour had passed before I received a call on my cell. Ron and I had stepped into Kristen's garage, so the children could not hear the conversations, and finagled various phone calls for the next hour or so. First, it was Amber. She had been allowed to use the phone. She was having a panic attack and wanted us to come get her. I tried to calm her and told her we would be right there. In reality, if we did go back to the Mission to get her we would be taking her to another facility, not home, but she didn't know that significant detail. I called Maureen who was elsewhere in the facility. She then located Amber, calmed her, and shortly called me back to let me know Amber was alright. Part way through those series of calls we also received calls from DHS. The caseworker informed us that a decision had been reached; the children would be placed with us. On that cold February afternoon, with Amber calmed and our phone calls ended, Ron and I clutched each other and thanked God for His goodness.

We stepped into Kristen's warm house and hugged our grandchildren: Kristen's three, and Amber's three who were now going home to live with us. We gathered them into the car.

"Where would you like to eat supper?" we asked.

"Steak and Shake!"

And so it was. A celebration at Steak and Shake. The evening was dark and dreary. We were worn and tired. But we celebrated three events: Mommy going to recovery, where she would get well; the kids coming to live with us; and Papa's birthday. Yes, it was Ron's birthday. His gifts this year were his daughter's temporary release from jail, the expectation of her healing, and three precious grandchildren coming to live with him!

When our two older children, Matt and Kristen, researched recovery facilities and decided upon the Kalamazoo Gospel Mission (KGM) for Amber they were quite adamant that Jesse not go to the same place. Research showed a lack of success when drug-addicted married couples entered the same recovery program. Rehabilitation was most successful when a person took responsibility for himself or herself, away from the proximity of the spouse who had once enabled him or her. Although the judge had recommended that Jesse go to the same recovery program, we encouraged Jake to take Jesse to another program, in another city. Jake trusted that the professionals at Kalamazoo Gospel Mission could determine if Jesse should be there with Amber and that the Lord would lead in the matter. We prayed with Jake about it.

The morning after Amber's panic attack, she again called us from the Mission. Seeing the caller ID, I was apprehensive to receive the call. I hesitated but answered the phone, not knowing how I would respond to her call of distress. This time, instead, I heard her pleasant and calm voice. "Mom. Late last night, they opened the outside doors and the homeless women from the city came into the halls. The workers put mats on the floor and the women slept on the floor outside my room. This morning, Mom, I showered in a group shower with about 50 women. I've never done that before."

Oh no, I thought. *Now she's going to want us to come get her.*

"And you know what, Mom?" she asked. "I love it here."

Three days after Amber entered the program, Jake took Jesse to meet with the counselors at the Mission. KGM is family-oriented and desire healing for the entire family. They accepted Jesse. Although the couple was separated for the first few days, they were united soon after in a family unit of the facility.

Theologian D.A. Carson wrote in his book *Jesus' Sermon on the Mount and His Confrontation with the World: An exposition of Matthew 5-10,*

> "The two terms [grace and mercy] are frequently synonymous, but where there is a distinction between the two, it appears that grace is a loving response when love is undeserved, and mercy is a loving response prompted by the misery and helplessness of the one on whom the love is to be showered. Grace answers to the undeserving; mercy answers to the miserable."

Certainly God's grace had answered to my undeserving self, and now God's mercy was answering to my miserable and helpless self.

And Jesus Whispered ~

I have heard your prayer, Kathi. I have listened to your cry for mercy. I am forgiving and good, abounding in love for you. In your day of trouble, you called out to me; I have answered, and I will continue to answer. I anoint you, Kathi. You will overflow with my goodness and mercy.

The Psalmist wrote, "Taste and see that the Lord is good. Oh, the joys of those who take refuge in Him."[75] We had taken refuge in Him. We had tasted of His mercy, and we had found the LORD to be good.

1. Near the beginning of this chapter, I explained my renewed understanding of God's favor to me and to my family. What insight about God's favor can you gain from the following passages?

Psalm 30:5

Psalm 84:11

Proverbs 3: 3, 4

Proverbs 3:34

2. In an earlier chapter, I shared my plans for Amber to receive counseling at a local clinic. Instead, she was arrested for her drug use, something I did not want to happen, but something that by God's mercy probably had saved Amber's life. In this chapter, I shared my desire for Amber to go to a lovely recovery facility; instead, the Lord led her to an unattractive facility in the rough side of the city. Again, God's mercy was evident, as The Kalamazoo Gospel Mission proved to be the best program for both Amber and Jesse. What circumstances in your life (or those you have observed in the life of a loved one) were not your intended plans, yet later proved to be evidence of God's mercy?

3. Read Psalm 25:6, Isaiah 63:9, and Ephesians 2:4. What do we learn about God's mercy toward us?

Now read Hosea 6:6, Micah 6:8, Matthew 12:7, and James 2:13. What are God's expectations of us regarding mercy? Why, how, and when should we be merciful to others?

4. As I wrote at the beginning of this chapter, I had accepted Jesus Christ as my Savior at the age of ten. In my late teen years, I became disinterested in the Christian life, but as a young mother, I turned back to the Lord and committed my life to Him. What about you? Have you ever received Jesus Christ as your Savior, truly accepting the finished work of Jesus Christ on the cross? Do you have assurance of salvation and God's love for you? If so, thank Him now for His wonderful gift to you. If not, or you are uncertain, consider making this prayer your heartfelt response of faith:

> "Heavenly Father, thank You for Your love for me, for sending Jesus Christ to die on the cross for all my sins. His precious blood washes me clean. You raised Him from the dead. He's alive today. And I thank You all my sins are forgiven. I'm righteous by the blood. I'm under God's favor. And I thank You Father that surely goodness and mercy will follow me all the days of my life from this day forth. In Jesus' name, Amen."[76]

What assurance do you find in Romans 8:1? Romans 8:35? Romans 8:37?

Read 2 Corinthians 5:21. How does God now see us? How does this make you feel?

What does Jesus tell you in John 10:29?

I especially want to lead you to Hebrews 13:5b. What has God promised you? How do you respond to this promise?

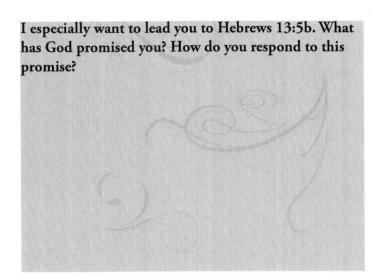

Now, pray, thanking God for these promises of His faithfulness to you!

chapter five

WHISPERS OF COMFORT
Seeking Peace within This Pain

*In sorrow and suffering, go straight to God
with confidence, and you will be strengthened, enlightened and instructed.*
~ST. JOHN OF THE CROSS (1542-1582)

After ten confusing and painful days, we brought the kids to our home. It was a dark, foggy, February evening but the house was warm and inviting. They hadn't yet seen the changes in Nana and Papa's house, the bedrooms that were now their rooms. They were delighted. Back and forth they flitted between the two rooms.

"Hey, Ben, did you see my huge closet?"

"Look at your bulletin board!"

"Where did you find these posters, Nana?"

But I think Ron and I were more delighted than they were. We didn't know whether they would be with us for a few days or a lifetime. It didn't matter. We wanted them. We wanted to protect them from all harm. We wanted them to grow closer to Jesus. We wanted them to know His great love for them.

One month before the arrest, our house had undergone some changes. I had shopped for and ordered new furniture. The carpeting was selected and I was ready to place the order when, well, you know the story. Now, we couldn't afford to continue the redecorating, so we cancelled the order, what we could cancel, that is. Some of the furniture had already been made. My beautiful, large sofas went into storage at the furniture store, and I didn't see the finished product for another 18 months. I wasn't disappointed. The beautiful fabrics, pieces, and carpets weren't important anymore. All that mattered now was our family, and particularly, the three young ones, ages 5, 9, and 13.

Now, the house suddenly became theirs as much as ours, and we let them know it. It was their home. They could have friends and cousins over to spend the night. Their video games were connected to the family room television. Hooks and shelves plastered the laundry room walls to hold their boots, shoes, and coats. Kitchen shelves were stocked with Natural Jif®, Frosted Flakes®, and Mrs. Butterworth's® syrup. Cookie Dough Ice Cream filled the freezer, and whole milk and Gatorade® packed the refrigerator. Jacob shared a bathroom with Papa, and Ben and Kaylee shared the larger one with me. They weren't weekend guests any longer—they were residents.

We drove the children to and from their schools, 25 miles away, frequently several times a day for after-school activities as well. I met with teachers and dentists. With doctors and caseworkers, in attempts to keep their everyday lives as normal as possible. We were all getting established in our new routine, and the kids seemed so pleased to be settled.

Three weeks after settling the children in our home, we celebrated Jacob's 14th birthday on a Friday evening. My brother, Larry and sister-in-law, Mardel, were with us for Jacob's cake and ice cream. I casually mentioned that earlier in the day a family acquaintance had commented about Daddy's health. "I'm sorry to hear your father is in poor health, Kathi," she had said. I assumed she hadn't realized the unfortunate progression of Daddy's dementia that had been occurring for months. When I looked at Larry's face, I knew it was even worse. This woman had known something about my own father that I hadn't known. Daddy was struggling. *I must go to him.*

Early the next morning, I took the children to Coldwater to meet their Poppy (Jake, their other grandpa), aunts, uncles, and cousins, to further celebrate Jacob's birthday and spend the night. I immediately drove to the nursing home and rushed to my Daddy's room, where I found him struggling to breathe. Larry sat beside him, holding his hand. My precious Daddy was dying. I knelt beside him and began to sing about the name of Jesus.

"He hears you, Kathi. He squeezed my hand when you began to sing."

I had not seen him since the arrest 2 ½ weeks before. Regrets entered my mind. I recognized them. They were not from God. They were from the enemy. I pushed them aside and continued to sing about Jesus—Daddy's Jesus, my Jesus. I sang through the day and most of the night. The name of Jesus consoled me as much as it comforted Daddy.

And Jesus Whispered ~

*When you don't know what to say or how to
pray, just speak my name. My name is power.
It is comfort. It is life and salvation. When
you speak my name, you open the floodgates
of your spirit, and the Father fills you with
the Holy Spirit, your Comforter.*

My sister, Becky, arrived from her home several hours
away. As morning light filled the room nurses entered and
left his room, saying goodbye to Wayne, my Daddy. Some
cried. Some talked to him. Some prayed. They loved him
too. Even throughout the weakest points of his life, he exemplified Jesus, and they were drawn to him because of it.

We brought Mama to the room. With help, she
pulled her weakened body up from the wheelchair and laid
it across his. I heard her whisper, "I wish I could go with
you." And I wished she could, too, not for my sake, but
for hers.

Matt Redman wrote the song, "Your Grace Finds
Me." I've often thought that God directed him to write
that song just for me for that morning I sat with my dear

Daddy when my heart was breaking into little pieces. Interviewed by Hannah Goodwyn of Christian Broadcasting Network (CBN), Redman said,

> "The song is an attempt to sing about the wide spectrum of God's grace. The grace of God found us at the cross—and that is the centerpiece of all we believe, but that is not the end of the story of grace. For His grace keeps on finding us—the undeserved goodness of God showing up in our lives. You can find it in the newborn cry and find it in the light of every sunrise. You'll find it in the mundane and on the mountaintop. And more to the point, it finds you."[77]

More to the point, God's grace had found me. As it had found me so many times throughout my life, it was in the light of this Sunday sunrise, and it was there in the sorrow shortly after, when Daddy took his last breath.

STRENGTHENED under the BROOM TREE

"Neighbors bring food with death," Harper Lee wrote in *To Kill a Mockingbird*. It was a line I had read dozens of times as I taught concepts from the novel to students of my classes. Now I found that statement to be true in my own experience. After Daddy passed and I'd made funeral arrangements, I came home to smell a warm peach cobbler that had been placed on my kitchen counter. A note was next to the large dish. My neighbor Mrs. Nickerson had brought it. She had reached out to us in our time of need. *I want to thank Mrs. Nickerson,* I thought. Two days later, ladies from our church brought a huge meal and set it out for our large family between the hours of funeral home viewing and visitation. I so appreciated their hands of service and their arms of love. They served the twenty people who had slept in our house and needed to be fed. I simply lacked the strength to prepare meals as I typically would. Just a day later, Mama and Daddy's church prepared a luncheon for our extended family and friends. Mrs. Nickerson, our church, and Mama and Daddy's church showed God's love to us.

Later, as I looked back and remembered the nourishment provided to us, I further connected to Elijah's experience. After learning of Jezebel's threats to kill him, Elijah had run for his life and hidden in a cave. On his way to the cave Elijah paused after a day's journey into the desert. Depressed, exhausted, and wanting to die, he sat under a broom tree and slept. An angel of the Lord touched Elijah and said, "Get up and eat."[78] Bread had been baked over hot coals. A jar of water was placed beside the bread. Elijah ate and drank. Refreshed but still worn and tired, he again slept. Again the angel touched him and told him to get up and eat. "The journey is too much for you," the angel added.[79] You see, God meets us at both our strong and our weak points, and in all times He provides for us. Although we might assume God had not directed Elijah to take this journey, God still provided for him. It doesn't matter if we are physically or emotionally or spiritually in a place He has led us. He will meet us.

The broom tree was more of a bush, with draping thin branches and narrow leaves like those on the weeping willow tree at the edge of my yard. But the shade of the small broom tree was enough to protect Elijah from the hot sun of day. In Elijah's time, the roots and branches of the broom tree were used for kindling. Because embers from its wood retained heat, desert travelers often covered the embers with a layer of sand, providing themselves a warm mattress on the cold desert night.[80]

When we are exhausted or depressed, God will strengthen and shelter us as He did Elijah. He will give us shade when we are traveling through the dry, hot wilderness. In God we can find warmth when we are cold and miserable. In God we can find nourishment when we are hungry and thirsty. In God we find communion, as His angels minister to us, like they ministered to Elijah, serving him the bread and water. Like Elijah, I was sitting under that "broom tree," my temporary place of refuge. The Psalmist wrote about the rest we can find in the shelter and shade the LORD provides:

"I look up to the mountains—does my help come from there? My help comes from the LORD, who made heaven and earth! He will not let you stumble; the one who watches over you will or slumber. Indeed, he who watches over Israel never slumbers or sleeps. The LORD himself watches over you! The LORD stands beside you as your protective shade. The sun will not harm you by day, nor the moon at night. The LORD keeps you from all harm and watches over your life. The LORD keeps watch over you as you come and go, both now and forever" Psalm 121 (NLT).

"Strengthened by that food [and rest], he [Elijah] traveled forty days and forty nights."[81] Women, especially and instinctively, are keen to other's needs for nourishment particularly during times of depression and exhaustion. Mrs. Nickerson and the ladies from the churches had reached out to my family and me in our time of need, supplying nourishment to our weakened bodies and weary souls. It was as though they said, "Eat, for the journey is too much for you."[82] At the time, the journey seemed too much. But we were strengthened under the "broom tree" and were equipped to move onward and face what would come.

Grieving with an Already Broken Heart

In spite of the pangs of grief that accompany death, the funeral was an awesome celebration of Daddy's life. We grieved as those who have hope![83] Amber and Jesse were permitted to leave their rehab program to attend the funeral. Our children and their families were all together. In addition to the touching message given by the pastor, Matt, Kristen, and Amber each gave homage to their grandfather. I gave a eulogy to my daddy. Lynette sang "Goodbye for Now." As she sang, I tried to make eye contact with her, smiling, to encourage her in this difficult task of singing lyrics that represented each of our inmost feelings. Even so, my heart broke more with each line I heard. Although many of the lyrics were sad to hear and to face, they nonetheless encouraged and comforted me. The truths were found in Revelation 21, where I read that "He will wipe every tear from my eyes, and there will be no more death or mourning or crying" (Revelation 21:4 paraphrased). I had to say *goodbye for now* to this man I loved so much, the first man I ever loved. The man who had taught me how to love. The man who looked like Jesus to me.

Matt had selected a song to be played at the end of the service. As we said our goodbyes, we listened to Chris Tomlin's, "Our God" and found ourselves worshipping our God, who had given us the wonderful man we called Daddy and Grandpa, the God who had restored Amber and Jesse to Himself and brought unity to our family, the God who would be with us and for us in the uncertain future we faced, and the God of all comfort.

And Jesus Whispered ~

I am greater than death and stronger than the enemy. I am your healer, Kathi. Nothing can stand against you because I am with you.

Later, I journaled about my loss.

Dear Daddy

Dear Daddy,

I sat beside you, singing, "Jesus, Jesus, Jesus; There's just something about that name," while you took your last breath. Larry, Becky, and I looked on, while Mama held your hand, our hearts breaking to let you go.

It was the greatest loss I'd ever known.

It was a day I had never wanted to live.

I knelt by your casket and sobbed. As the days passed, I thought I had cried so much that I couldn't cry any more, but I did cry again.

The crying continued. For a long time. I mourn you. I yearn for you.

I'm remembering a Daddy who made Christmas fun and who gave me beautiful Valentines. I'm remembering a Daddy who brought us kids running when you emptied the noisy change out of your pants pockets on Friday evenings after work.

I'm remembering a Daddy who sat at the table late in the evening and ate Mom's homemade bread soaked in cold milk.

I'm remembering a Daddy who worked all week long—then spent cold winter Saturdays cutting, hauling, and stacking firewood to heat the big house throughout the coming week.

I'm remembering a Daddy who bought a new camera to take pictures of his daughter, the homecoming queen.

I'm remembering a tender-hearted Daddy who mourned the loss of his own father and his mother, his brothers and sisters and brothers-in-law and sisters-in-law, and on and on. A compassionate man whose heart ached for those who were hurting. A man who wanted to do good for others. A man much like Jesus. So I know you understand how I'm feeling now, Daddy.

I will continue to miss you and mourn you, but I will also find joy and delight in the memories. I will strive to carry on those special customs and traditions you began in me and in my family: the love of nature and of the simple life, the love of family and neighbors and friends, and the love of Jesus and those He came to save.

I will watch Jacob mowing the lawn, *your* lawn, with the John Deere, *your* John Deere. I will watch Benny playing in the woods by *your* lane. I will watch Kaylee riding her bike around *your* driveway.

I will watch the eastern sky and as I watch, I will listen for the *shout* when our Lord will bring you and will catch me up to join you. We'll all be together again. Goodbye until then, Daddy.

Your little blonde girl.

We were Daddy's family. His life went on in us. After the funeral, my family kept me going. The grandchildren kept me strong. Our daughter and son-in-law faced prison time. I was hurting, and I was grieving. But there was much to be done: forms to complete, death certificates to obtain, daily routines to be maintained with the grandchildren. So I kept mercifully busy.

Since the time Daddy and Mama had left their big yellow house, I knew that it couldn't sit empty. The bills continued to come in. We needed to rent the house to cover our expenses, yet, as I wrote in an earlier chapter, the house was run-down and needed much work to make it rentable. Daddy had served in the Army Air Force during WWII. A few months earlier I had completed stacks of forms, had made hours of phone calls, and had finally found Daddy eligible and approved for a VA (Veterans' Administration) pension that could be used to make improvements in his home. He qualified for retroactive pension of approximately $14,000, yet it would take considerably more paperwork and time to receive that retroactive payment. Ron and I discussed the matter with my siblings, offering to put our own money into house repairs to be reimbursed when the promised VA pension was paid. My siblings agreed. Ron and I put $14,000 into house repairs, to bring the house to a rentable standard. The VA consistently postponed and delayed the claim until Daddy died. Then the VA dismissed the retroactive pension claim. Ron and I had no hope of receiving the money we had put into repairs for the yellow house.

I spent as much time as possible with my mother at the nursing home. She had lost her husband who had been her lifeline and her reason for living. Her face and demeanor revealed it. Her beautiful blue-gray eyes held no trace of the spark they had displayed for nearly nine decades. Her sisters often visited her at the nursing home filling in the gaps when neither my brother nor I could be there. She had twelve healthy days after Daddy passed. Suddenly she was in the hospital, struggling to breathe and suffering more than she ever had in her past travails. My brother, sister, and I were with her round the clock. The doctor soon brought news we dreaded hearing: no more could be done for our precious mother. Larry made the decision to have her moved back to the nursing home, the closest thing to her home in those last ten months. The nurses and aides welcomed her, bathed her, and tended to her needs like she was their own mother. I journaled:

Sunday—Oh, no!

Four weeks ago today, my daddy died. Today, I sit at my mama's bedside, watching her shallow, limited breathing. She is comfortable, though, and for that, I am thankful.

Monday—Closer to the Arms of Jesus

I am watching my mama getting closer to the arms of Jesus. Of course, I've been talking to her. I've told her I think she and daddy will have a big yellow house together like the one they loved here for so many years. I imagine what it will be like. When she steps through the door, she'll see a large picture window overlooking a garden (like the Garden of Eden) filled with red poppies, birds, and deer. I think she'll have that summer kitchen she's always wanted, with the cook stove, a vintage green and creamy white one. I think the stairway will be open with a beautiful railing. And I think she'll find Daddy sitting at the table. He won't be reading his Bible as he was in his big earthly house because The Word Himself will indwell the entire space. Instead, Daddy will jump up and run to meet her at the door. They'll hug and dance while the angels sing and rejoice. Best of all they'll see their Savior and drop to their knees and raise their hands in praise. They'll recognize all who've gone before them who are in the presence of the Lord and they'll celebrate together until we join them. These years were not enough. This lifetime is way too short. It is so obvious to me now that God made us for eternity, and I'm so thankful for eternal life.

On Tuesday, the third day, I continued journaling and posted a response on Facebook to the many wonderful friends who had reached out to me, answering questions they had asked and trying to convey my appreciation to them:

Jesus weep, the others observed, "My how Jesus must have loved him!"[84]

And seeing me weep, I can imagine Jesus observing, "My how she loves her mother." Then I can see Jesus doing for Mom what He did for Lazarus, saying, "Margie, come forth."[85] And Margie will step right into the arms of Jesus.

I am remembering my Savior's love and compassion. And remembering His great power of resurrection, I can once again change my focus from watching my mother die or watching my mother suffer to watching my mother prepare to leave my arms for the arms of Jesus. His grace is sufficient.

In my darkest moments, the Word uplifted me: "Even in darkness, light dawns for the upright.[86] Because of the LORD's great love, we are not consumed, for his compassion never fails. It is new every morning. His faithfulness is great."[87] Wednesday was a new day for me and I knew it would be a glorious new day for my mama.

The sun was shining. Evidence of spring saturated the outdoors and permeated the halls of my mother's nursing home. I neared her room, and my heart wrenched as I saw the hospitality cart outside her door, a sight I remembered one month ago. This lovely collection of cookies and orange juice, coffee and fruit was notice that the family would need sustenance as we would watch and wait.

Several of us were there—my sister and brother, some cousins, my aunts and uncle, and my little Kaylee. It was the grandchildren's spring break from school. Jacob and Ben were spending a couple of nights with their cousins. Kaylee had stayed with me and now her youthful vibrancy was a delightful contrast to the death that loomed in this hall and in this room. She bounced back and forth between her great-grandma's bedside and the chapel in the next room where her coloring books were spread out. We adults went in and out of Mama's room. Heads slowly shook in sadness and in heartbreak. Aides and nurses came in and stood by her bed. They cried. I loved them for it. We could do no more to keep her here with us. My mother was dying.

She had put up a good fight. She certainly had not been created to die, which was most obviously detected in her steadfast resolve and perseverance through the years. God had originally made her for eternity. Death is the sad result of the story of the Garden of Eden, of sin, and of death. It's the story of a body that should have been perfect and could have been perfect. It's the story of a downward spiral of health problems and of a broken spirit, especially in the last month.

For years, she had plodded forward—literally plodded forward. Her crippled feet and shrunken stature, stenotic spine and withered muscles, cancered blood and arthritic bones impeded her once-vibrant step, year by year, month by month, and day by day. Only one purpose kept her going—Wayne. She couldn't leave him. He needed her. "Til death do us part," they had promised. And the love grew stronger than the promise. So she loved him and served him until the day he didn't need her any longer. That day was one month before.

I joined Mama in those last steps of her dying. As much as I could from the outside looking in. This was Mama's dying, not mine. I was alive and being alive made it all the more difficult to accept this separation that death was about to force upon us.

She turned her head and looked at me. She spoke. Soft. Single. Syllables. I couldn't hear or understand her.

Then no more movement. Eyes closed. She lay perfectly still. Not in sleep. But in the stillness that sometimes comes before death. This was a stage of death, one I'd witnessed in my Daddy one month prior, one I did not want to face again. A double-edged blade was stabbing the tenderest place of my heart. She would never look at me again. She would never speak to me again. I yearned to hear her voice, even those soft, single, syllables I could not understand. I wanted to place my ear close to her mouth and listen closely.

I'm tired. I want to go back. To yesterday. To last week. To last year. I want to listen to my Mama. I want to listen and soak up her every word. Please God, can we go back?

But there was no going back because this dreadful parting that was coming about between a mother and a daughter was death. Death had been compounding itself in my Mama's life for many years. Death had been initiated and implemented in a beautiful Garden of Eden, and it had ruined every life since. It was aging and suffering, cancer and illness, war and killing. It had parted many mothers and daughters, and it was strong—stronger than I could fight. And so I sat beside Mama and watched as she lay still, her body dying.

Suddenly, the stillness was broken by an occurrence that became a ritual of the next hours: she opened her eyes and turned her face upward, lifting her purpled, bruised hands straight from her elbows, toward heaven, toward her Savior. I watched this sacrament in amazement.

Please, God, let Mama's body die so her soul can go to You and to Daddy.

I had prayed for a visible sign of Mom's soul leaving her body.

It would be such a simple thing for You to do, Lord God.

I didn't *need* a sign to know that my Mama was going to the Lord Jesus. I simply *wanted* it. And knowing that He cared about my wants and desires, I prayed.

She dwelt in this last state of her physical being, one I had not yet observed in these days of watching her die or in the weeks of watching her struggle to breathe or in the years of watching her vibrant body deteriorate into the broken woman who now lay before me. Mama simply turned her right hand away from the sterile white sheet and raised her palm toward her Savior as she took her last breath.

I opened the Bible, the Word. I went to the Psalms and discovered that Mama had lived the Word in her death: "Yet I am always with you. You hold me by my right hand. You guide me with your counsel, and afterward You will take me into glory . . . earth has nothing I desire besides You. My flesh and my heart may fail, but God is the strength of my heart and my portion forever."[88]

He had held her by her right hand and had taken her to glory. He had answered the simple prayer of a simple daughter. And I knew that the Word would help me face life without her, that God would be the strength of my heart and my portion forever, and I understood a bit more about death and felt a bit less of its sting.

And Jesus Whispered ~

She's here, Kathi. Can you hear the angels rejoicing? Your Mama's death is precious in the Father's sight.

Suddenly I was an orphan. We once again went to the funeral home and made arrangements. The time came for Mama's viewing. I continued to journal:

Friday - I Remember Mama

Yesterday was a tough day. Last night was agonizing. I couldn't imagine facing a day of my life without her.

Early this evening I went to see her body—my Mama. I went early, before the others. I wanted my own time. I needed my own time.

I push my way up each step and through the foyer of the familiar funeral home. Grief presses me back. I know this grief quite well now, and I hate it. My neck feels swollen. My ears feel plugged. My throat makes sounds I don't recognize. I press forward into the big room, my eyes set on the silver box, the one we selected yesterday or the day before. I don't remember which day. Time is of no consequence now. My eyes flood but I see her through the tears. She is resting on pink satin, laid out in the dress we selected, the one she purposely left behind in her Sauder© closet the day she left her house for the nursing home. She wears the new creamy-white sweater Becky bought her. She wears her Barbara Bush pearls. She is so pretty. *Did I tell her recently how pretty she is?* I close my eyes and I feel her tucking me into bed at night. I smell the Ponds® Cold Cream on her soft skin. I remember her in the kitchen, making her yellow Sunbeam rolls. I see her dancing down Main Street in Disney World. My heart is full, and it is breaking; my mind is worn but it is sated with Christmases and snuggling and her voice singing me to sleep and the melodies from her lips as she flits through the house.

How much time passes, I don't know. I return to the present time, opening my eyes and looking around the room in this funeral home, a place I don't want to be, facing what I am facing. I hear voices. People have now filled the room. My grown children are here. My neighbors and friends are here. Now the room has taken on a different countenance. Instead of the parlor of death, it has become a playroom filled with my little grandchildren. Their animated voices and their healthy little bodies, full of young life, proclaim that their great-grandma, my Mama, lives on in them.

My friend, Carrie, encouraged me this evening. "Life is amazing," she said, "and we are a part of it." Yes, Carrie, life is truly amazing. And I am a part of it because of my precious Mama. Now I will carry on what she began: I will tuck my little ones in to bed, I will pass on the tradition of baking the yellow rolls, and I will dance down Main Street.

Tomorrow I must say goodbye. I know it's her body, that her soul is in heaven and that she will receive a new, vibrant, healthy body. But it's her old body and her touch and her voice that I will miss. It's the smell of Ponds® Cold Cream and of yellow Sunbeam rolls baking in her oven. And I will always remember my Mama.

Tomorrow did come. The day to say goodbye. The sun was shining through the trees. I said, "Honey, look at the beautiful sunrise. 'Even in darkness, light dawns for the upright.'"[89] My heart was breaking, but I remembered God's promises. We woke our children and dressed to go to Mama's funeral.

Jesus had called me blessed: "Blessed are those who mourn for they shall be comforted."[90] Comforting arms surrounded me from the moment I walked in the door of the funeral home and continued to surround me all day. Friends and family lavished their love on my family and me. They were the comfort of Christ to me. I felt the hands of Christ all day as people ministered to me. I was broken, but God's grace was sufficient, and my shattered heart welcomed it.

In the service, Lynette sang of the "Amazing Grace" that had saved us and now had found us in our weakest moments. Our children and nieces gave tribute to their grandmother. I spoke her praises. The little ones bounced around all day, laughing, dancing, and playing together. It was a constant reminder of Mom living on in our family through her children, grandchildren, and great grandchildren. We followed the white hearse carrying Mama's body, her coffin encased in pink lilies, in the funeral procession to the cemetery. The back seats of our car were filled with little grandchildren. "Curious George" played on the DVD player. This had not been planned, but God used it to bring joy to my heart. The procession paused in front of the big yellow house, as it had one month before, when we brought Daddy home to his final rest. Now, the hearse carried Mama around the circle drive one last time. It took her past the spirea bushes, not yet budded on this early spring day; past the front steps and porch, where the straw broom hung as though waiting to be used; near the old dinner bell; and then back past the mailbox, crossing the road to the cemetery. It was the same route we had taken Daddy, one last time around the drive of their lifelong home.

We buried Mama next to Daddy, at the cemetery across the road. The sun was shining. The birds were singing. Her soul was in heaven. Our precious nine grandchildren stood behind me as I sat across from the casket (or her basket as my little Kaylee called it) at her burial. I could literally see Mom's life continuing on in my life, in my children's lives, and in my grandchildren's lives. All was well with the world. But early in the evening, after most of our family had gone home, I suffered the greatest grief I have ever known. Ron tried to comfort me. "It's okay, honey."

"No, it's not okay," I responded.

I didn't want to burden the children by seeing me in this deep grief. Ron held me as we walked outside in the fresh air, down the country road, while I sobbed and cried out to God. I knew God's peace and comfort was available to me, but I didn't feel it. I *couldn't* feel it at the time. But He was definitely still there. I began repeating, "I love you, Lord." Over and over I said it, placing my focus on my love for Him, realizing that He would comfort and fill me with His love. Peace came in the midst of my grief, and for that, I was thankful. Ann Voskamp's words, in writing about the passing of her friend, Kara Tippetts, described the quiet communion I had with the Lord in those moments and in the days to come: "The strange hush about things now, in the wake of her really going, feels like a lingering holy."

And Jesus Whispered ~

I will heal your broken heart, my child.

I told myself that others grieve more deeply—perhaps over a younger life lost. But grief is grief. And comparing it doesn't lessen one's grief. Each life matters to God. Each grief matters to God. My grief was deep, encased in my already broken heart, but my God was sufficient even at grief's worst point. He patiently walked beside me during my suffering. As I had found his grace in the sorrow when Daddy passed, I again found it on this day I buried my mother and in this darkest evening of my soul. As I had heard in a song I so loved, I intentionally breathed in His grace and breathed out His praise, over and over, until it became a regular practice in my daily life.

My friend Mandy suffered extraordinary grief in losing her mother. Mandy's father had passed away some years earlier. Pam, Mandy's mother, was a vibrant, active person. She and Mandy, an only child, were not only mother and daughter but were best friends, as well. When Pam passed away after an extended bout with cancer,

Mandy was certainly grief stricken. We friends saw a Mandy who appeared to be ably coping with the loss of her mother. But few people knew of the additional burdens of regret Mandy carried. Being a parent's health advocate is a blessing the child can give back to the parent in the last years of his or her life, but after the parent passes, the adult child often has regrets and guilt about caring for the parent. I certainly did. And Mandy did. Although Mandy did the best she could for her mother, she later questioned some of her choices and decisions made in her mother's behalf: *Why didn't I make mom have that test earlier? Should I have helped her chose a different doctor? Or treatment program?* Additionally, Mandy had been carrying an extra burden for quite some time; her daughter who lived several states away was in the beginning states of a divorce, and was parenting Mandy's only grandchildren. The situation doubled Mandy's sorrow. Two years after losing her mother, Michelle's grief still existed; she felt lost without her mother and sensed a hopeless future. Mandy's grief was compounded by her own guilt and by family problems.

Losing a parent differs from person to person. Many factors enter into one's grief. About two years before my father passed away, as his health was diminishing and I was facing the future without him, a co-worker and I conversed about taking care of our elderly parents. Her father who recently passed away had lived out of state, and she had rarely seen him. He had been in a nursing home and her sister was his health advocate. She said, "I never shed a tear. I hadn't been close to my father and never truly noticed his passing." I was dumbfounded and carefully tried to conceal it. Certainly many elements comprised her grief or the lack of it. A lifetime of them. I was sad for her that she hadn't experienced the blessing of loving a wonderful father like mine. I knew that grief was not something I could or would avoid. It meant I had someone to love, and I had loved and lost two someones.

Was my grief worse than another person's grief? Was it worsened by the earlier crises in our family? In her book, *When I Lay My Isaac Down,* Carol Kent wrote, "There is a common ground of understanding, forgiveness, acceptance, and healing when we are authentic with each other." She suggested that when we share our stories of suffering, we needn't try to figure out whose suffering is worse.

"We are all suffering to one degree or another. Is the woman whose husband betrayed her by having an affair with her best friend hurting more than I am? Is the man who is choosing to keep his marriage vows to a woman who is too self-centered to consider his feelings and needs in less emotional pain than I am? . . . Is the couple who lost their home and had to declare bankruptcy due to corporate downsizing in worse straits than I am? . . . Is the woman who just gave birth to a child with Down['s] Syndrome in more anguish than I am? . . .

"The bottom line is that it doesn't matter. We are all a bunch of flawed human beings living in an imperfect world. . . . We don't need a meter to tell us which pain hurts the most. All of our heartaches produce great sadness, and telling our stories to each other brings a release, a comfort, and the knowledge that somebody cares."[91]

Sharing our grief experience is consoling. It doesn't matter what factors into that grief. The important thing is that we let ourselves experience grief and that we welcome others to share their grief, as well, hoping to console their breaking hearts.

Death was not in God's original plan, not a part of the life He had planned for us in that beautiful garden. But Adam and Eve chose sin. Death followed. Consequently we all know the grief suffered by every human being since. And since we know that God works all things for good to those of us who love Him,[92] it is not surprising that He turns our wretched grief into consolation for others. It seems to be a process similar to our present-day practice of paying it forward. We drive through a McDonald's lane, place an order, and discover that the person in the vehicle before us has paid for our meal. We appreciate it, and we likely pay it forward to the car behind us, or pay it forward in another manner in the near future. So it is with the comfort and consolation our heavenly Father has bestowed upon us in our darkest moments. When we receive that comfort, we, in turn, can pass it on to others. Why? Because now we understand their pain. That compassion and comfort overflows from our hearts to others. I've paraphrased 2 Corinthians 1:3-7, which teaches that concept.

> *Praise be to the God and Father of our Lord Jesus Christ, the Father of compassion and the God of all comfort, who comforts us in all our troubles, so that we can comfort those who are going through any trouble with the comfort we ourselves have received from God. For just as the sufferings of Christ flow over into our lives, so also through Christ, our*

comfort overflows. If we are distressed, it is for the comfort and salvation of others; likewise, if we are comforted, it is for the comfort of others and it causes us to be patient and to endure the same sufferings of others. Just as we share in sufferings, we share in comfort [paraphrased].

And Jesus Whispered ~

As you suffer, Kathi, I want you to share in the sufferings of others. As I comfort you, Kathi, I want you to comfort others. Let my comfort overflow in your heart and be poured out to others. Be patient with others as you share in their suffering and in their comfort. Now you understand what they are going through. Turn your grief into consolation for others' comfort and for their salvation.

In her book, *Wounded by God's People*, Anne Graham Lotz described a time in her life in which she found herself in a spiritual wilderness.

"If I could have pinpointed one particular trigger that launched me into my wilderness experience, it would have been my mother's departure for heaven. Not only did my grief leave me with a feeling of emptiness and deep sadness, but there were many circumstances around the time of her death that seemed to drive me into a spiritually dry, barren, lonely, rocky place. Life seemed to close in on me . . . One morning, I was especially conscious of the oppression and darkness that seemed to be crushing my spirit . . . my eye fell on this verse, "The people remained at a distance, while Moses approached the thick darkness where God was."[93] . . . The verse . . . leaped up off the page as I heard God whispering to me . . . *Embrace the darkness* . . . God is in the darkness and God is in the wilderness. . . . And if I can't turn to Him there, who can I turn to?"

Anne further shared that some of her pain was the result of her own poor choices; some was due to the emotional and spiritual wounds inflicted upon her by others; but it was the passing of her mother that left her in a spiritual wilderness.

My, how I could relate to her, and I'm sure many of you can, as well. Sometimes life closes in on us. The passing of my parents was not unusual at their age, but compounded by the devastation of our daughter's arrest, impending prison sentencing, and other wounds. I was suddenly in a vulnerable position that made me feel isolated and separated from God. His Word told me otherwise. He was there with me in my wilderness, my darkest places, and He would never leave me nor forsake me.[94] I had experienced His grace and His mercy. Now I was experiencing His comfort.

> *Grief is like a long valley, a winding valley where any bend may reveal a totally new landscape.*
> ~C.S. LEWIS, *A Grief Observed*

My grief was like the long, winding valley about which C.S. Lewis wrote. Throughout my valley with its many bends, I processed my grief while journaling. I share one of those entries here.

Dear Mama

Dear Mama,

I miss you, Mama. Your battered, navy blue, leather purse is still on my closet floor, unmoved since I brought it home the day you passed. I looked through it recently, handling every piece within, from Altoids® mints to your ink pens. I read every little note you had written and cherished your scratchy handwriting we always teased you about. Then I browsed through one of your diaries, one from ten years ago, and wished we could be back there again.

Occasionally, I look in the mirror and catch a glimpse—of you, Mama!

I haven't erased your messages on my answering machine, Mama, but I haven't been able to listen to them, either, for such a long time now. I think I'll try again in a few days. As much as it hurts, I want to hear your voice again.

Oh, how I long to be held in your arms. Now you understand how things are here and there. Speaking of the Word, do you read it there? Do you speak it? Or sing it? Or since Jesus is the Word, does He totally indwell you? You must love it there. Well, anyway, I'll bet you miss me. You don't miss being here, even though you loved the place: the country, the yellow house, the garden, the land.

The yellow house has been painted. I was so careful to select the right yellow, and I think it's perfect. Then I had all the spindles on the porch rail, the spindles that have sat in the shed for 30 years, put back on the porch where they belong.

And oh how pretty the new porch light looks. I occasionally leave it on overnight—so I can look over there and see the light. Reminds me of you, expecting someone to drive in. Just to think of the years you left the porch light on, waiting for Larry, or for me, or for Becky. Little did I know then that I would do the same thing with my children.

And as much as you loved the yellow house, Mama, I'll bet you don't really miss it, either. I'm sure God has given you a new yellow house in heaven, and it has the open stairway you always wanted and the summer kitchen with the green and cream-colored cook stove. And Daddy shares that yellow house with you.

You're both with our Savior, Mama. What peace you must finally have. That peace is beyond my comprehension. I'm always striving for it here. I write about it sometimes. It's so difficult to be steadfast, but I keep trying. As much as I look forward to seeing you both, I know the first and foremost joy will be seeing my Savior, Jesus. I can only imagine what it is like. I'm so happy for you, and I can hardly wait to be with you and Daddy there someday. Hug Daddy for me. I miss him so much. Tell him I'll write him soon, and I'll write you again after I listen to your voice on the answering machine.

With love,
Your honey girl.

GLEANING BITS of JOY in the MOURNING

Within the year after Amber's arrest and the passing of my parents, the birth of two new grandchildren brought joy into our shattered world. Through the birth of these two little boys, I recognized a pattern I had observed through the years in our large, extended family. My father was one of twelve siblings and my mother was one of eight. Within the year of a family member's passing, a new baby was born. It wasn't that the new life replaced the one that went to heaven, but it was a sign of the family continuing, of life going on. It was a refreshing bit of joy in the midst of the mourning.

All men are like grass, and all their glory is like the flowers of the field; the grass withers and the flowers fall . . . but the Word of our God stands forever (Isaiah 40:6-8).

I didn't like the change death brought into my already shattered world. It was difficult for me to imagine a future without grief. But I wanted it. I yearned for it because the present was ceaselessly painful. I noticed in the Old Testament that a time was set for mourning and then the people moved forward. The Israelites grieved for Moses "thirty days until their time of weeping and mourning was over."[95] I chose to look for joy in the midst of my mourning, for "beauty instead of ashes," for "gladness instead of mourning," and for "praise instead of . . . despair."[96] It was God's promise for me. In my journal postings, I began to move from grief into the joy to be found.

The Poppies of the Field

Daddy's and Mama's garden amassed poppies at a certain time of each summer, beautiful red poppies. Likewise, Daddy's and Mama's lives amassed vibrancy. Their beautiful lives honored and served God.

Passersby stopped their cars. Some actually drove in the driveway and knocked on the door. "May we look at your flower garden?"

But now the poppies are gone. For a few years, a little stem here and there popped up. Nothing remains of the vibrant red poppies. Instead, withered stubble covers the ground.

I am reminded of what I've read in the Bible, "All men are like grass, and all their glory is like the [poppies]. But God's Word stands forever."[97] God's Word is powerful. It is mighty. It is beautiful. It is amass with the vibrancy of life. I will open the Word and let it fill me. I want people to stop and look at my life to see the beauty.

Grief to Beauty

I went to the grave this morning to replace the once-pink geraniums and the withered vines with a mum plant. This mum burst with soft purple blossoms, one I knew Mama would have loved. I hadn't been to the grave in weeks, an unusual break of custom for me. After months of faithful visits, often crying and reminiscing while I tended and watered the summer greens, persistent grief had encompassed me, a grief I had been trying to shake by avoiding the custom. But on this beautiful autumn morning, I faced my grief to bring beauty.

The little country cemetery was peaceful. Sunshine flooded the diamonded dew. As I opened the hatch gate of my car, two wild turkeys descended from the low limbs of the bordering maples, their flapping wings breaking the stillness of the quiet setting. I lifted the plant and mustered the few somber steps to the site. *Together Forever*, the stone read, the words entwined in a heart joining their names Wayne and Margie. "Mama, Daddy," I cried, as I had so many times before.

The flag waved on Daddy's side of the gravesite, and I remembered the military gun salute the local veterans had given Daddy before he was buried. My pride for him momentarily surpassed my grief. Stepping behind the tombstone, I discovered that since my last visit, a bronze plaque had been set in place by the Veterans Administration to honor Daddy. I pulled out my cell phone and took a picture of it to send to my sister. It wasn't until after I printed the picture that I saw the rays of sun flooding over the tombstone and into my lens.

On this beautiful autumn morning words of the poetic prophet Habakkuk described the setting at the gravesite,

> *His glory covered the heavens and his praise filled the earth, His splendor was like the sunrise; rays flashed from his hand, where his power was hidden.*[98]

I considered the splendor of this morning and the sun rays that flashed from God's hand. I was reminded of his power, the power that lifted the souls from Daddy and Mama's aged bodies; the power that will one day lift those broken bodies out of that grave and transform them into perfect bodies; the power that will bring us all together again; His divine power that "has given us everything . . . and has given us his great and precious promises,"[99] and the power that now consoles my grief to bring beauty.

A New Path
Now, my journey is taking me down a new path, and how I'm learning that a part of the journey is moving on.

It's a dreary, rainy, late October morning. The sun is not shining. The trees are no longer covered with brilliant foliage. One might think I'd be depressed today but I'm not. The same grace God has rained down upon me in the past is pouring upon me today. It's not a cold rain like I would feel outside today; it's a warm, refreshing rain, and I'm basking in it.

As I prayed this morning, I looked across the yard at the yellow house, as I often do, and again I thanked God for the heritage bestowed upon me by my parents. This time, no lump comes to my throat nor do tears well in my eyes. Instead, I see a path ahead that is bright and sunny, and as I step onto the path the rain of grace soothes and heals. I read from Proverbs.

"My daughter, keep your father's commands and do not forsake your mother's teaching. Bind them upon your heart forever; fasten them around your neck. When you walk, they will guide you; when you sleep, they will watch over you; when you awake, they will speak to you. For these commands are a lamp, this teaching is a light, and the corrections of discipline are the way to life."[100]

God leads me on the next path today. If you've grieved you'll recognize the paths. This one is refreshing. The beautiful part of the journey is moving on.

I thought I couldn't live without him, but now I know I can. That would make him proud.

~OSKAR SCHELL,
speaking about his father, in the novel,
Extremely Loud and Incredibly Close

And Jesus Whispered ~

I am a father to the fatherless, my child, and I will comfort you as your mother did. I love you with an unfailing, unconditional love, even greater than that of a parent. You are mine, Kathi, and I will take care of you.

Jesus-Whispers for You

1. You may have noticed how music spoke to me in my grief. How does music speak to you? What songs in particular?

2. Elijah rested under a broom tree where he was strengthened and nourished. Where have you collapsed to find strength and nourishment? Read Psalm 34 and Psalm 35. Note the common thread woven as the passage begins (Psalm 34:1) and ends (Psalm 35:28). Write what Jesus whispers to you in this passage.

3. I wrote letters to both my mother and my father after they passed. It made me feel as though I were speaking directly to each of them. Do you need to speak to someone you've lost? Do you have a message yet unspoken? Perhaps a confession to be made or forgiveness to be granted? If so, write a letter to that loved one.

4. The Bible tells of the many wonders of heaven. What do envision heaven to be?

5. Again in this chapter I wrote about the wonderful heritage my parents had given to me and to my siblings, now passed down to our families, a heritage of love and faith in the Lord Jesus. If you have had a similar heritage, write a prayer of thanksgiving. If you have not, study Ephesians and Isaiah 56:13-17. Then write a prayer of thanksgiving for your wonderful heritage in the Lord, one that you can pass on to your children.

6. In her book Wounded by God's People Anne Graham Lotz asked her readers some stirring questions that I think we should all ask ourselves when life has crashed in on us. "Deep down in the hidden chambers of your soul, are you offended by God? Angry with Him, even? Are you wandering from God? You thought you knew Him, but now He seems remote at best." Write a response. Openly share your feelings with God.

7. In Extremely Loud and Incredibly Close, young Oskar Schell struggled through his process of grief. Toward the end of his struggle, he said, "I thought I couldn't live without him, but now I know I can." Write about times you've felt both ways: (1) that you can't live without him or her; (2) reaching points that show you can live without him or her.

chapter six

WHISPERS OF HOPE
Renewing Our Strength through Soaring Hope

*It was one of those March days when the sun
shines hot and the wind blows cold: when it is
summer in the light, and winter in the shade.*
~CHARLES DICKENS, *Great Expectations*

L ife roared. The arrests of Amber and Jesse were made in February. My father had passed on a March morning three weeks later. A few days later my mother lay in a hospital bed struggling to breathe. My March days were like those Charles Dickens described—hot and cold, light and dark. My emotions went back and forth as often and as quickly as the warmth of the sunlight changed to winter in the shade. Those changes came as rapidly. I needed to discover the treasure of *light* in its fullness, all day, every day even in my time of mourning. Ecclesiastes is clear that there is a time to mourn and Romans 12:15 commands us to weep with those who weep, but 1 Thessalonians 4 urges us to grieve as those who have hope. Because our hope in in Jesus the Light.

After He created the heavens and the earth, God spoke and light came to be. In Genesis, we read that "God saw that the light was good, and he separated the light from the darkness."[101] Darkness can be good (or *very* good as God said in Genesis 1:31) because it is our time to rest in sleep. Darkness brings dew to refresh the grass and cooler temperatures for plants to bloom. But darkness can hide the truth from us and leave us feeling alone, separated, and afraid. Yet, no matter how dark a situation we believers face, God still brings light to it. He fills us with the light of knowing His glory as we look on the face of Jesus. He is our *treasure*. Paul tells us about our treasure in 2 Corinthians, "For God, who said, 'Let there be light in the darkness,' has made this light shine in our hearts so we could know the glory of God that is seen in the face of Jesus Christ. But we have this light shining in our hearts, but we ourselves are like fragile clay jars containing this great treasure. This makes it clear that our great power is from God, not from ourselves (2 Corinthians 4:6, 7 NLT).

In his expository "Notes on 2 Corinthians 2017 Edition," Dr. Thomas L. Constable identifies the treasure I held in my fragile jar of clay, "The 'treasure' that every Christian possesses is 'the knowledge of the glory of God' (v. 6, i.e., the gospel). Even though this is what dispels spiritual darkness, God has deposited this precious gift in every clay Christian ('earthen vessels') . . . God has done this so all may see that the transforming 'power' of the gospel is supernatural ('of God'), and not just human."

Knowledge of His glory, spiritual darkness dispelled, and transforming power—these treasures were all in my broken, earthen vessel. This treasure had been easily discernible in the light. But during times of darkness, I truly discovered its value.

"Although we were like sacred gems to the Lord, the enemy wanted us to think we were of no value" (Lamentations 4:1, 2) [paraphrased]. These words described how we looked at ourselves, "How the gold has lost its luster, the fine gold has become dull. The sacred gems, you and your family, are scattered at the head of every street. The precious son and daughter of Zion, Ron and Kathi, worth their weight in gold, are now considered as pots of clay, the work of a potter's hands."

In his "Notes on Lamentations," Dr. Constable explains the demise of the sacred gems, "The gold and precious stones that had decorated the temple no longer served that function. They now lay in the streets of the city defiled and dead . . . The enemy had regarded the citizens of Jerusalem, who were more valuable to it than gold, as worth nothing more than earthenware pots . . . [and] had smashed many of them."

Our enemy, Satan, was trying to make us believe that we were worthless and hopeless, broken earthenware pots to be discarded. Jesus told me otherwise.

And Jesus Whispered ~

You are precious in my sight, Kathi. You are worth more than your weight in gold to me. I am the potter; you are the clay; I will never discard you. I suffered to make you flawless. I have restored you to myself. Do not lose heart.

In spite of the crises in our midst, Ron and I discerned God's power working within us, enabling us to continue pressing forward. As the passage in 2 Corinthians 4 continues, it perfectly described our journey. "We are hard pressed on every side, but not crushed; perplexed, but not in despair, persecuted, but not abandoned, struck down, but not destroyed. We always carry around in our body the death of Jesus, so that the life of Jesus may also be revealed in our body" (2 Corinthians 4:8-10).

Moment by moment, hour by hour, day by day, light to dark, or dark to light, the knowledge of the glory of God kept us from being crushed, lifted us out of despair, protected us from abandonment, and healed us when we were struck down. Why? Because when life roars, Jesus whispers.

I often prayed the Word of God, a habit I had begun within the few years leading up to our crisis. In those years of learning to pray the Word, God had prepared me for this present time when my mind sometimes could not formulate even a simple prayer. His Word most often became my prayer.

Surely the Psalms were the "right speech" for my prayers. They were most often the words I would have wanted to compose, if I could have. God had transcribed them for me, knowing I would be praying them back to Him. I usually paraphrased the verses to match our life situations, as I poured out my heart to Him.

O Lord, so many things are against us! They rise up before us! Many are saying, "God will not deliver Kathi and Ron, Amber and Jesse. But you are my shield, O Lord.[102]

Summon your power, O God;

Show us your strength, as you have done before.[103]

You break down gates of bronze and cut through bars of iron.

You have sent forth your word and healed Amber and Jesse.
You rescued them from their destruction.[104]

As I prayed the Psalms, He spoke them right back to me.

And Jesus Whispered ~

I hear your words, Kathi. I consider your sighing. I listen to your cry for help. In the morning, I hear your voice as you lay your requests before me and as you wait in expectation.

I prayed the New Testament as well. Frequently, I prayed aloud, while walking through the house, driving in the car, or while browsing the aisles of the grocery store. Romans 10:17 tells us, "faith comes from hearing the message." I wanted to hear the message of God as I prayed. Speaking and hearing the Word increased my faith and trust in Him. Because my fears could be so overwhelming, I personalized the words of 2 Timothy 1:7, which became a regularly spoken prayer of the Word, "God, you do not give me a spirit of fear, but you give me a spirit of power, and a spirit of love, and a spirit of a sound mind" (NLT paraphrased). Over and over I quoted those words, which still compose one of my most common prayers of the Word. The prayer reminded me that my fear was not from God. Because it was not from God, I knew it was from the enemy whom I continually rebuked.

Finding Power in the Treasure

The spirit of fear was not from God. God gave me a spirit of power, and I yearned for all the power He had to offer me. I read more about His power in Ephesians 1:17-21, another passage which has become a prayer for my family and me.

"I ask You, glorious Father, God of our Lord Jesus Christ, to give me the Spirit of wisdom and revelation, so that I may know You better. Because the eyes of my heart have been enlightened, I pray that I might know the hope to which you have called me. I pray that I might know the riches of your glorious inheritance for me. I pray that I might know Your incomparably great power for me, a believer. That power is like the working of Your mighty strength, which You exerted in Christ when You raised Him from the dead, and seated Him at Your right hand" (NIV paraphrased).

Ron and I didn't know what the future would hold, but we trusted in God who would give hope and riches and in His incomparably great power, all because of our standing in Christ and all a part of the treasure we carried in our broken jars of clay.

And Jesus Whispered ~

You are hard pressed, but, Kathi, do not be crushed. You are perplexed, but do not despair. You are persecuted, but I have not abandoned you. You are struck down, but you are not destroyed. I have made my light shine in your heart, Kathi, to give you a glimpse of my glory. You'll always see it when you look in the face of Christ.

In Scripture, anointing with oil represents refreshment and joy. The host often poured oil on the head of a weary traveler, a guest in his home. The anointing is considered by some to be a picture of God's bestowal of the Holy Spirit. I reflected upon the anointing from the Lord, in the familiar passage of Psalm 23. "You anoint my head with oil" (Psalm 23:5). And in Psalm 92, I read of an anointing I hoped was in my future: "Fine oils have been poured upon me. My eyes have seen the defeat of my adversaries . . . The righteous will flourish like a palm tree, they will grow like a cedar of Lebanon; planted in the house of the Lord, they will flourish in the courts of our God" (Psalm 10b-13).

Oh, how I yearned for that anointing. I visualized the Lord pouring those fine oils upon me, a clay vessel, my adversaries having been defeated and my family flourishing like a palm tree planted in the house of the Lord. I wanted God's anointing drenching and filling me with hope, riches, and His transforming, supernatural power. I wrote about it.

Anointed with His Treasure

My Lord lifts the jar and pours the oil upon me, anointing me with treasure. I'm praising. This enables me. I'm thankful. This blesses me.

He pours it upon my head. I'm discouraged. He makes my face shine. I'm saddened. He gladdens my heart.

The oil of gladness refreshes my weary body. I'm hurting. He heals me. I'm grieving. He consoles me.

It is a fine, sacred oil. I'm homesick. He comforts me. I'm famished. He fills me.

It is the oil of joy. I'm anxious. He gives me peace. I'm suffering. He fills me with hope.

His treasure saturates me. His anointing never ends. He never runs out.

So it is with His treasure. He saturates us with light of the knowledge of His glory to show that the power He gives is from Him, not from us.

In *Pursuit of His Presence*, Kenneth Copeland suggested that since the word *Christ,* a Greek translation of the Hebrew word *Messiah,* translates into English as anointed or The Anointed One, we should naturally translate the word *Christ* into The Anointed One and His Anointing every time we find it in the New Testament, as it brings new meaning to each Scripture. The fact that we are Christians means that we are anointed like Him.

The Bible tells us that God anointed Jesus with the Holy Spirit and power,[105] and that I also received power when the Holy Spirit came upon me[106] when I was saved. As a believer, I "have an anointing from the Holy One," and I "know the truth."[107] In the difficult March days and in the weeks and months that followed, the truth of God's incomparably great power was evident to me.

I've heard people ask widows, "How are you doing?" Their replies most often are, "I'm taking one day at a time."

I understood their response, as best I could. By His power, Now I was taking one step at a time, one day at a time.

The children brought joy into our home and that joy refreshed. When I was busy with their activities and taking care of them, I spent little time in worry or fear or grief. But occasionally, on the weekend, the children went to Jake's house. Then I found myself weeping, my body releasing emotions that had built up for days. Everything was different as I wrote in a blog posting.

These Days

These days are different. I was an organized person before, but, these days . . .

Nothing is ever finished. I feel like I'm never completely prepared to teach. One day I had all my papers graded—in all classes. But I kept thinking something was missing. It was. My preparation for my online class hadn't been completed. My students were online two days later, but I had nothing prepared for them.

The house is a mess. It's upside down and inside out. My spring cleaning isn't done. I can't walk in a straight line through my storage room. A path had to be plowed for the Direct TV® installers. Tubs from the Amber and Jesse's house. Boxes from Mom and Dad's house. Clothing is piled. In the washer. In the dryer. Across the bed. I sort the children's seasonal clothes. It adds one more tub. I file the funeral papers. It adds one more box to the collection.

Furniture is dusty. Woodwork is dirty. Blinds are broken, light bulbs need replaced. Box elder bugs are invading.

I forget to study for my weekly ladies' Bible *study*.

My heart wants to invite guests to dinner; my body can't get the house cleaned.

I start a job but rarely get it completed before I'm forced to move on to another.

Suddenly, I can't find my Bible, my devotional book, or my journal. Oh, there they are! I open my journal and reflect upon what God has said to me this week.

On Monday, God told me that I need to continue to give to the Lord and let that gift be one of honor, not talking unbelief as I give it but rejoicing when I give it. He said, "If the willingness is there, the gift is acceptable."[108]

On Tuesday, God told me I can expect the glory of God's presence because I'm "justified by faith," so I have "peace with God through our Lord Jesus Christ . . . [and] access by faith into grace."[109] I know He certainly has shown me His grace throughout the last months.

On Wednesday, God told me that I am not supposed to fear the enemy because I am "more than a conqueror through him who loves me."[110]

On Thursday, God told me that I "have this treasure,[111] that the excellency of the power may be of God, and not of me."[112] During *these days*, I want to see Jesus within me and know that everything I need is within me because that's where Jesus is. I want to experience the "excellency" of His "power."

And on Friday, God reminded me to hide His Word in my heart.[113] I started hiding His Word in my heart when I was a young girl. At that time, it was easy to memorize God's Word. I learned Psalm 119:11 as a song, "Thy Word have I hid in mine heart that I might not sin against Thee" (KJV). These days, it's more difficult to hide it, to memorize it. These days, I need to read it often to keep it hidden in my heart.

Now it's the end of the week. The house is still a mess. Several jobs are still undone. But these days, and with every fiber of my being, I need to hide and speak Words of faith.

So from an enlightened perspective, after digging into the Word of God, I concluded that these days really were no different. The same Jesus was with me in light or dark, in peace or in trial, and He is the same yesterday, today, and forever.[114] I continued to hide His words in my heart.

I was their Nana, but I mothered my grandchildren. I loved those parts of motherhood that were protective and nurturing: preparing nutritious meals, providing cute clothes, snuggling, helping with homework, cheering at the baseball games. Other parts of motherhood were more difficult for me: doctor appointments and vaccinations, dental appointments and fillings or extractions. Of course, I wrote about the bad along with the good.

Free Yourself from the Chains, O Captive Daughter

The sun is coming out this morning. I've had a rough night, dreading taking Benny to the dentist. I pleaded, and then remembered that I don't have to plead. So I've asked God to heal Benny, to keep him from pain through this ordeal that is before him: having two teeth extracted and one filling. Why do I struggle so with trusting God in it? God has reminded me that He loves Benny more than I do, that He loves Jacob more than I do, that He loves Kaylee more than I do, that He doesn't want them to hurt, that by Jesus' stripes, Benny is already healed from his hurt.

I've gone to the Word this morning, reviewing Isaiah 52, 53, and 54. I am immediately exhorted to "Free [my]self from the chains on my neck, O captive Daughter of Zion."[115] And this is what I pray for and trust in.

"How beautiful on the mountains are my feet; My God reigns!; I lift up my voice and shout for joy . . . the LORD comforts me . . . all the earth will see His salvation (He saves me); I must be pure – for the LORD will go before me, the God of Israel will be my rear guard."[116]

Today, He will go before me and prepare the office, the dentist, the assistant, the meds, and the procedure. He will be Benny's and my rear guard. I will trust Him.

FINDING HOPE in the TREASURE

Ron and I held the treasure God gave us. The power He gave us was most obviously from Him, not from us. We knew His presence in our darkest moments and He reminded us of this in His Word. Amber and Jesse's earthen vessels were filled with treasure, as well, revealing God's transforming, supernatural power. Their changed lives evidenced the miracle that continued to amaze us. Therefore, we were learning about the hope to which the Lord Jesus Christ had called us (our prayer from Ephesians 1). The passage in 2 Corinthians 4 reminded me not to lose heart, as well, "Therefore we do not lose heart. Though outwardly we are wasting away, yet inwardly we are being renewed day by day. For our light and momentary troubles are achieving for us an eternal glory that far outweighs them all. So we fix our eyes not on what is seen, but on what is unseen. For what is seen is temporary, but what is unseen is eternal" (2 Corinthians 4:16).

God was renewing us through hope. We were fixing our eyes on what we could not see. As I read the Bible, new insights that I had never before seen became clear while reading the same words I had read many times throughout my life. Was this the "Spirit of wisdom and revelation," for which I had prayed, so that I could "know him better?"[117]

Was it God highlighting the words I needed to see at this time? I believed it was. What a loving God I had, who would give me this wisdom and revelation so that I could "know Him better"[118] and "know the hope to which He had called"[119] me.

> *God is the only one who can make the valley*
> *of trouble a door of hope.*
> ~CATHERINE MARSHALL

The Mission had strict rules, and Amber and Jesse followed each one. DHS had even stricter rules; Amber and Jesse respected those as well. They were determined to honor the Lord; honoring others was a natural reflection of this honoring process.

In Amber's first weeks at the Mission, her counselors had to hold her back. She was so excited about the way the Lord had changed her life that she naturally wanted to share it with others. In one of our conversations she told me about a young woman, Darcy, who had entered the Mission. Her face was battered and bruised. After recently beating Darcy, her boyfriend had been arrested on a drug charge and was presently in jail. Amber reached out to Darcy, telling her how much God loved her and had a better plan for her life. Sadly, within a few days, this woman's boyfriend had been released on bail and she left the Mission. Amber was upset and disappointed that Darcy had left the safety and strength found within the walls of the Mission. Amber's counselors told her there would be a time in the future when she could and would minister to others in need, but in this present time Amber needed to heal and recover. I was so proud of my daughter. I was awed by the new Amber, the Amber I hadn't seen in nearly twelve years.

We were amazed to observe Jesse as well. We had never known this Jesse. He spoke of the Lord as if he had known Him for years. He thirsted for God's Word. His sister soon looked to him as the spiritual leader in their family. A new believer herself, she sought his advice and counsel on her new life in Christ. She and the rest of Jesse's family were finding new and great hope in their treasures.

The first six weeks of the program were the same for anyone who entered the Kalamazoo Gospel Mission. The Life Application was an in-depth examination of the individual's relationship with Jesus Christ. We took the children to the Mission and celebrated their parents' graduation from this phase of the program. Then they began an intense recovery program, including marriage and individual counseling.

DHS was leery of allowing the kids to see their parents at the Mission, as the Mission was filled with a rough group of broken people. Other residents looked upon Amber and Jesse with wonder. Here was a couple married 15 years, with three children, whom they had together. It was quite unusual in the Mission setting. But Amber and Jesse had been as broken as everyone else who entered that Mission. Ron and I were now also broken. No façade remained of the candy-coated lives we had lived for so many years. I doubted that any façade would ever cover us again. We were all a rough group of broken people loved by Jesus.

Meanwhile, DHS made regular home visits to our house. We also met with them in their offices. Ron and I were required to attend classes to maintain our foster license. These requirements were some of the most humbling circumstances I've ever experienced, particularly being told how to care for and raise *my* grandchildren. But I cooperated. We did not want to begin the probate challenge of becoming custodians of the children without DHS involvement, so we continued to be their foster parents through DHS. We developed and maintained a trusting relationship with our caseworker. Frequently in our meetings a caseworker or her supervisor would warn us that most often, even after completing a rehab program, the drug addict will return to the drug. We needed to prepare ourselves for this, they said. Each time one of them told us this it felt like she had stuck a knife in my stomach and twisted it. I immediately became nauseous, and the nausea remained, sometimes for days. I found my way out of this by speaking and believing God's promises, by regained the assurance His Word provided. *My daughter is healed by the stripes of Jesus. Jesse is healed by the stripes of Jesus.*

DHS wasn't the only place where the enemy attacked. He shot those fiery arrows in the court rooms; from local television, radio, and newspaper reports; and from friends and acquaintances. Some people felt compelled to continually remind us that 90% of all drug addicts go back to the drug. Percentages varied according to the reports. "It's only a jail-time conversion," said a former jail deputy. "I've seen it many times." The shield of faith became my armor to extinguish those fiery arrows.[120] Speaking and believing God's Word reminded me of His faithfulness and increased my faith. I spoke the Word in my writing, as well.

I Dig Deep

Summon your power, O God; show us your strength, O God, as you have done before. Rebuke the beast.[121]

Bad news is frightening. The enemy makes me forget the Lord's faithfulness; the bad news pierces the knife into my stomach. I'm suddenly nauseous. Discouraged. The outlook is not good. It's negative. Depressing.

I dig deep into the Word. Dig deep to remember my heritage, to remember the heritage of my family, the heritage that belongs to my children. I dig deep into the Word that is near me. God is in my heart. He placed His Word there when the righteousness came by faith.

And once again, I know the strength God gives, the strength to stomp on the fear. I remember the strength He has given me before, and I remember His faithfulness. The Word tells me,

"All your sons will be taught by the Lord . . . great will be your children's peace. In righteousness you will be established. Tyranny will be far from you; you will have nothing to fear. Terror will be far removed; it will not come near you. If anyone does attack you, it will not be my doing; whoever attacks you will surrender to you. See it is I who created the blacksmith . . . who . . . forges a weapon. . . I have created the destroyer to work havoc; no weapon forged against you will prevail, and you will refute every tongue that accuses you. This is the heritage of the servants of the Lord."[122]

Attack is not from God; in fact, any who attack will have to surrender to God. God created the one who forges the weapon. Their weapons will not prevail against us. Only what God wants will prevail. I am desperate for Him at this time.

And so I pray, *Summon your power, O God; show us your strength, O God, as you have done before. Rebuke the beast.*[123]

And Jesus Whispered ~

I have redeemed your children. I have healed them. My faithfulness is your shield. No weapon will prevail against you, Kathi. Don't believe the words of the world. Believe and trust in My Word only.

We attended Probate Court hearings regarding the children and District Court hearings regarding the criminal cases. Amber and Jesse were given permission, by both the Mission and their court officers, to leave the Mission and attend these hearings. At each criminal case hearing the judge, satisfied that the couple was in recovery, delayed scheduling the sentencing. I wasn't sure of the legal implications but the attorneys said it was a good sign. An amazing moment happened at one of the first hearings. After his conference with the prosecuting attorney Amber's attorney met us in the hall with a document in hand, outlining the legal charges. He used his pen to draw large X's through several of the charges. "The prosecutor has dropped these charges," he said. "Just one felony and one high-court misdemeanor remain. Amber won't be sent to prison now. Jail is a strong possibility, but not prison." I wanted to hug him. My shoulders and chest relinquished a heavy weight, and I felt like I could breathe for the first time in months. Tears welled in Ron's eyes. We left the courthouse crying, *Thank you, God.*

And Jesus Whispered ～

I have gone before you. I am the one who breaks down gates of bronze and cuts through bars of iron. I have called you by name and will bestow on you a title of honor.

Jesus had whispered to me through his Word, Psalm 45:2-4. I was amazed. A title of honor? For me? For Ron? For Amber? For Jesse? I began to understand what it meant to be chosen, to be adopted by God the Father. I belonged to Him. What great hope I had!

The children's lives were as normal as they could possibly be, under the circumstances. We loved them unconditionally, and they knew it. My protective Nana Bear nature was tested and tried in the first few weeks. Jacob, a bright eighth grader, was not doing his best in his health/science class. I called the teacher to find out why. It seems he had refused to complete an in-class assignment, which had resulted in 0%. His attitude about the assignment was poor, she said. Then, on the following day, he did poorly on another, resulting in 10%.

"What were the dates of those assignments?" I asked. The dates she gave me were the two days following his parents' arrests.

"And what was the subject of those assignments?" I asked, already knowing, as I held the two papers in my hands.

"The Dangers of Methamphetamines," she replied.

Any thirteen-year-old would have struggled with writing about the crime for which his parents had been arrested. My heart hurt for my grandson. My mind went back to the ten years I had taught at this grade level, remembering the pain forced upon so many of my students by the poor decisions or criminal offenses of their parents. I had comforted so many of them and had adjusted their assignments in their times of distress. *Certainly she doesn't realize what happened to him.* I thought. But when I asked her if she knew what had happened to Jacob on the days of those assignments, her response was, "Yes." She continued, "If the assignment was upsetting to him, he could have asked to leave the room."

My mind flooded with thoughts. *Leave the room? Ask in front of the other students? Under his circumstances?* Her tone was demeaning. Her condescending comments indicated that she thought poorly of Jacob, his parents, and of me. I wanted to scream at her, but that would not have honored Jesus. So I calmly showed her respect and reiterated a statement I had made at the beginning of the conversation, "We expect Jacob to be respectful with you."

"Yes," she replied. "But he wasn't."

And Jesus Whispered ~

I am near you when you are brokenhearted, and I deliver you when you are crushed in spirit.

The grandchildren's honeymoon at our home had ended a few weeks after the children came to live with us. They realized Nana's and Papa's roles had changed from what they were previously accustomed. Now there were rules and curfews and chores to be done around the house. But we determined to shower them with love. The children were happy, strong, and healthy. They flourished.

We kept a growth chart in the doorway of the laundry room. Smiles lit their faces each time they were measured!

Despite the love in our home and the happiness we shared we all had our times of brokenness. One day Jacob sat on his bed and cried. "I want things to be the way they used to be," he said. I held him, cried with him, and let him know I understood. And sometimes, when Ron was at work, the kids were in school, the house was quiet, and I was alone, fears and discouragement filled me, as well. Again I poured the treasure, the knowledge of the living God, upon my broken vessel. I exposed my vulnerability and failures in my later writings about one of those times.

It's My Party and I'll Cry if I Want to

I had a party today. Sorry I didn't invite you, but I was all caught up in myself. This kind of party is much more fun when I'm all alone.

It started this way, Surely God is good to me but I've stumbled and lost my footing. All day long I'm plagued with trials; seems there's a new problem every morning. If only I had said something different. If only I could explain. If only he truly loved me. If only she understood. If only things were different. If only. (Based upon Psalm 73:1-2, 14-15).

The party was really getting going at this point. (Maybe you should have been there!) When I tried to understand all that was going on, I found it oppressive. By this time, the enemy was knocking so loud at my door. He really wanted to come to my party.

Like I said, I wanted to be alone at my party. But I did recognize that malevolent knock, so when he became oppressive to me, I left the room where he was knocking. I entered the sanctuary of God (based on Psalm 73:17). It's a quiet place. So comfortable. Such a place of refuge. God took my right hand; He became my strength; and I realized that I desired nothing more than to be with Him. (based on Psalm 73:23-25). It was good for me to be near God. He said, "You can have great peace because you love my law, and nothing can make you stumble" (based on Psalm 119:165).

And I said, "I wait for your recovery, O Lord, and I follow your commands. I obey your statutes, for I love them greatly. I obey your precepts and your statues, for all my ways are known to you." (based on Psalm 119:166-168) (That last part made me realize that He had known about my party all along.)
Looking back on it, I see it really wasn't much of a party at all until I entered His shelter. That's when the true celebration started.

Next time I'll try to have a different kind of party—in the sanctuary—and I will invite you.

The children had finished their school year in Bronson, about 25 miles away. Their summer was filled with baseball games; visits with Poppy Jesse's family; family vacation at Maranatha with us, their cousins, and aunts and uncles; and regular visits with their mom and dad. DHS gradually increased the time allowed. The visits most often took place at our house or Jake's, and we occasionally took them to the Mission to visit their parents. In the fall, they began the new school year in Quincy. Of course, changing schools is challenging under any circumstances. We helped the kids get to know other kids from Quincy before school started. Jacob had two kinds of ear infections days before school began. We attended open house, and the children met their teachers. We all had a good outlook on it, but they were a bit nervous, as I was that first day.

First Day of School

Today was the first day of school. New school for the kids. Mom and Dad aren't taking them this morning. I am. So I'm feeling a bit sad about it. For them. For their Mom and Dad. And for me. Jacob's doing well, I think. Will his ear hurt at school? Is the ear infection worsening? Or is it clearing up? Should I make a doctor appointment after school? Will he lose his only key for his locker padlock?

Benny wants me to walk him into the building, up to his classroom, but he doesn't want his sister tagging along. So he opts out and decides to make the trek himself, the long trek to a new classroom in a different school without his lifelong friends. All the other kids know how

183

to go through the lunch line. They know which foods are part of the school lunch. They know which foods are á la carte. Five minutes before we left the house this morning he showed me the papers the teacher gave him at open house last week. A reading survey to fill out. Directions for the first report, "What I Did during My Summer Vacation." Oh, well, I assure him the teacher will gladly receive those assignments tomorrow instead. He makes the trek alone to his 5th grade classroom on the second floor.

Slowly, slowly, I proceed down the street to the elementary school where countless cars are creeping along, their drivers seeking parking spaces. Parents are walking their children to the building. And so we, in turn, find a parking space and I walk Kaylee toward her classroom. "Oh-oh. We forgot your lunch." A panic-stricken look envelops her face until I add, "I'll bring it back before 11:00. No problem, Honey." We enter her brightly decorated classroom. She loves her new teacher but she looks down ready to cry. I whisper, "Can I hug you before I leave, or don't you want me to?" She shakes her head, *No*. So I take my hand away from her sweet little shoulder and say goodbye.

I step out of the room and peek back, knowing she will be fine in the care of her teacher, hoping she won't cry, like I am.

It could have been different this morning. Mommy and Daddy could have taken their children to school on this first day. They are nearby, in town for a probate court conference this morning. But DHS has their rules. How many times I've questioned these rules. Is this really in the best interest of the children? I pray. I remember that I have already committed all these issues to the Lord. I commit them again. I remember that I trusted Him in all. I trust Him now. I remember that He spreads His protection over them (my grandchildren), that He blesses the righteous, and that He surrounds us with His favor as a shield.[124]

I'm headed back to the elementary with Kaylee's lunch now, and I'm thankful for a future hope.

> *There is surely a future hope for you, and your hope will not be cut off.*
> Proverbs 23:18

The kids adjusted well to the new school year. Our evenings were filled with activities: homework; wrestling practice. Regular bedtimes were vital. I was insistent they had good meals and snacks. Our fall routine was established, and we were doing well. Amber and Jesse were in the last weeks of their recovery program, to be completed in late October. Their sentencing would soon be scheduled. I tried not to think about it.

The phone rang one day that fall. It was a caseworker from DHS in another county. A complaint had been filed against Ron and me. *What?* I thought. *Certainly this must be a mistake.* I couldn't wrap my mind around it. After her patient explanation, I understood the gist of the situation.

Weeks ago, at the end of the summer on our way to our Maranatha vacation, we attended Jacob's playoff baseball game out of town. We then left him in the care of Jake overnight, a completely acceptable occurrence as Jake was approved to have the children in his care. Jacob spent the night at a hotel with his Poppy Jake and the rest of his baseball team. Then Jake drove him to Maranatha to meet up with us all for the week's vacation. During the overnight stay at the hotel, Jacob met with his parents, Amber and Jesse, when he wasn't supposed to. Our caseworker from DHS blamed us. In fact, our caseworker had asked me about it the following week. I had told her the details and thought it was settled, but evidently it wasn't.

Now an outside caseworker had been assigned to review the complaint. She informed me she must make a home visit to our house, question the children privately, and meet privately with me. All of these meetings took place on a warm, September school evening. First, the caseworker met with the children in the family room. Then I met with the case worker on the porch so the children could go back to their after-school routines of homework in the house. Kaylee kept coming to the porch door, asking me when we would have supper. I disliked the children's routine being interrupted as it was. Within the week two other DHS workers came with the children's original caseworker during her regular visit. I resented DHS for making them meet new workers. It was all such an intrusion on their lives like big neon letters flashing, *We don't live normal lives. Our parents were arrested. Strangers control us.*

This complaint was simply another hurt, another fiery arrow from the enemy—not from DHS, but from Satan. The next morning, I received a text message and video link. "Listen to this song, 'Always,' by Kristian Stanfill," a friend suggested, unaware of the inner battle I was fighting. But God knew, and He sent a message in song—the exact words I needed to hear. "Always" and other songs based on Scripture spoke to my heart and helped me focus on Jesus.

Jesus had spoken to the enemy, "Away from me, Satan!"[125] "Get behind me, Satan!"[126] So I followed His example and spoke to the enemy whenever I realized he was shooting fiery arrows of resentment, fear, or other elements of darkness. I often walked through my house, jogged down the lane to our woods, or simply stepped onto my back porch, yelling, "Get behind me, Satan!"

The Mission began to permit Amber and Jesse to leave for scheduled visitations with the children. As the weeks progressed and the parents proved themselves trust-worthy, DHS gradually increased the time allowed with the children. From the first Sunday she entered the program, Amber had been allowed to go with her sister Kristen to Radiant Church. Jesse joined her as soon as he entered the program. They soon considered Radiant Church to be their home church. It was their place of worship, renewal, and hope. In time, Amber and Jesse were allowed to keep their car at the Mission and drive to the church.

Throughout their recovery program, Amber and Jesse were also allowed to leave the Mission for court appointments—Probate Court regarding the children and District Court regarding their criminal charges. The District Court continued to postpone their sentencing, as the judge was pleased with their continuing success in the recovery program. This was a promising sign to me, an indication that perhaps the judge was considering substituting their recovery time at the Mission for jail time. But of course I knew little about the legal happenings in District Court.

What I did know was that our daughter and her husband evidenced a changed life in Jesus Christ, unlike any I had ever personally observed. Near the end of their program, Amber gave me a copy of a letter she had written. The letter revealed parts of her own battle, and it evidenced the armor of God she had used to fight it, armor detailed in Ephesians 6:10-18—the belt of truth, the breastplate of righteousness, feet fitted with readiness, the shield of faith, the helmet of salvation, and the sword of the Spirit. Here is her letter to meth.

Meth,

Where do I begin? The first time I tried you I felt so strange. I didn't like the feeling so why did I try again? Oh, that's right, it was an attempt to fit in. Imagine that. I actually thought I could fit in when I included you. Funny isn't it how it ends up being exactly the opposite of that? At the end of our time together I wouldn't even answer the door. I felt like I was stared at if I went anywhere, and couldn't even talk on the phone in fear of someone finding out you were my only priority.

In the beginning, I remember the rush we would share. It was great being able to get all my cleaning done, do the laundry, and still have time for myself. But it wasn't long before it was just a game of tag, chasing you for the same rush. I sat day and night with you looking for anything close to the feelings I used to get from you. Days, weeks, months, years, how was it possible? I had so many plans, goals, projects that you were the center of. Where did all the time go? Eight years of my life, thinking pretty soon I will be done with you. I would tell myself, *anytime now I will let meth go and move on with my life.* But the *lies* always hovered above me; it was as if a dark raincloud was following only me! The *lies* like, *I can't do anything without meth; I am a loser anyway, so I might as well try to feel good; I can control it; Nobody really knows; I can still be a good mom and wife; Nobody cares about me.* I don't know why I continued to listen to your *lies* for so long. It was like a deep hole that the rain from your raincloud kept filling up. I was drowning and you couldn't care less.

But the entire time I was with you, on the other side of your raincloud, was my Savior. He was reaching His hand out for me, never tiring, in case I wanted to grab hold and let Him pull me out. Out of your hole of deception. Little did I know, with help from Him, I could break through your raincloud and step into the shining light. Without doing anything to deserve it, I was saved from *you.* He was there all along, My Lord and Savior Jesus Christ. There is no feeling you can give me that He can't trump. There is no *lie* that you can tell me that He can't crush. I am in His hands now, meth, so I am sorry to say I will no longer be playing that game of tag with you. And happy to say, it is bright sunshine where I am now. That raincloud you have reserved for me, well let's say you can cancel the reservation; I will never need it again.

Good riddance,

*Princess Amber Modert
(*My father is the King of Kings)

Late in October, Amber and Jesse graduated from the recovery program and left the Mission for good. It was a huge change for them. They lived with Jake, and they both worked his lawn service business. Then the court scheduled the sentencing for Monday, November 19. Anxiety crept into my being. Jesse's dad, Jake, and Ron and I thought Jesse would mostly likely be sentenced to jail, as Jesse had a prior misdemeanor. But I couldn't comprehend the possibility of Amber serving time in jail. *Surely God wouldn't let it happen. How difficult it would be for the children to have* both *parents in jail. What purpose would it serve? Why would the judge separate her from her children, especially before Christmas?* I thought perhaps he might sentence Amber but count her time in the mission as time served. In another scenario, I considered him giving her only 30 days in jail. In my mind, I formulated a plan: She would be released December 19, shortly before Christmas. My mind was crammed with thoughts, and each thought created more angst. There was no figuring it out. There was no answer. The decision was not up to me. But I could certainly see God's hand in every detail leading up to the sentencing, and I knew His hand would be upon the sentencing, as well. He used others to minister to me in this time of fretfulness. My website blog writing revealed some of my inmost thoughts.

God Is Using You

I am he who will sustain you. I have made you and I will carry you; I will sustain you and I will rescue you. Isaiah 46:4

If you've followed my postings, you know this is a trying time for me. Waiting. Wondering. Praying. Fearing. Trusting. Crying. Praising. I wait for Monday. And as I wait, God uses you to comfort and wait with me. To pray, to trust, to cry, and to praise with me. God is using you. It started with a Facebook message, a "Like," an "I'm praying for you." Then a phone call. A blog comment and an offer of prayer. An email from a student, *I'm praying that God will strengthen you.* It continues with a note from a sweet cousin, *Praying for Monday.* A dear friend delivers a hand-painted poppy. It ends with, well, it doesn't end.

It doesn't end because God says His purpose will stand. He summons a bird, or a man or a woman to fulfill his purpose. And He has summoned you for His purpose of comforting and consoling me. And you have answered Him. It's all a part of His plan for you, for me, for Amber, for Monday.

And aren't you glad that He makes the plans?

"I am God," He says. "And there is no other; I make known the end from the beginning . . . I say: My purpose will stand . . . I summon a bird . . . from a far-off land, a man to fulfill my purpose. What I have said, that will I bring about; what I have planned, that will I do. Listen to me, you stubborn-hearted, you who are far from righteousness. I am bringing my righteousness near, it is not far away; and my salvation will not be delayed. I will grant salvation to Zion, my splendor to Israel."[127]

Salvation and His splendor to Kathi and to her Facebook friends. To her Pastor and to her sweet cousin. To her blog follower and to you.
God is using you. And because He is, peace fills me now. If only for today, it is refreshing.

TAKING off MY SANDALS

In the days before the sentencing, I studied from the book of Joshua. One passage in particular, stood out to me. It was about the Lord's plan to do amazing things for the Israelites. The nation of Israel was ready to cross the Jordan River. The day before the crossing their leader Joshua gave the people orders, "Consecrate yourselves, for tomorrow the Lord will do amazing things among you."[128] This wouldn't be a river crossing like we know today. There were no bridges, no pontoons, no ferry boats. Instead, the Lord commanded Joshua to instruct the priests who carried the ark of the Lord, known as the Ark of the Covenant, to set foot in the Jordan River, at which time, He promised the waters would quit flowing. To make this even more miraculous the river was at flood stage!

The next day, in obedience, the priests stepped into the waters. The waters quit flowing. Creation itself obeyed the LORD. The priests actually stood firm on dry ground, right in the middle of the Jordan, while the whole nation of Israel crossed on dry ground. It was amazing. Can you imagine? I considered Joshua's order to the people given prior to this miracle, "Consecrate yourselves."

Consecration. Merriam-Webster online dictionary defines the word consecrate as "being set apart for a sacred purpose." In his book, *Draw the Circle*, Mark Batterson wrote, "Consecration is complete surrender to the lordship of Jesus Christ . . . It's letting God do for us what we cannot do for ourselves, and that's how God gets all the glory."[129] Being set apart for a sacred purpose. Giving God all the glory. The idea of consecration was suddenly humbling. In Paul's letter to the Corinthians, I read, "As God has said, 'I will live with them and walk among them, and I will be their God, and they will be my people. Therefore, come out from them and be separate,' says the LORD."[130] Those Words, God's Words, kept me desirous of consecration. I was humbled to realize that God would live and walk with me, that I would belong to Him. Mark Batterson further suggested that "if we consecrate ourselves to God, amazing things will happen. It's absolutely inevitable. Consecration always ends in amazing."[131] I wanted to be consecrated, to be associated with the sacred. I wanted the Lord to do amazing things, not only in the courtroom but in the lives of each one of my family.

After the incredible crossing of the Jordan River on dry ground, the Israelites faced another huge, unimaginable task—to bring down the city of Jericho. They would bring it down with a shout, making Jericho totally vulnerable to Israel's army. But before this was to happen, Joshua saw a man in front of him, a man with a drawn sword in his hand.

> *"Joshua went up to him and asked, "Are you for us or for our enemies?"*

"Neither, he replied, "but as commander of the army of the LORD I have now come." Then Joshua fell facedown to the ground in reverence and asked him, "What message does my Lord have for his servant?" The commander of the LORD's army replied, "Take off your sandals, for the place where you are standing is holy." And Joshua did so."[132]

Joshua's clearly recognized the authority of this commander, so much that Joshua fell face down to the ground in reverence. Shortly thereafter, Joshua referred to the commander as Jehovah.[133] He then inquired of the LORD, wanting to know the Lord's will for himself, "What message does my Lord have for his servant?"

Commentator Matthew Henry's explanation of this passage created in my mind a picture of Christ leading the battle we had been in now for many years, most intently for the last ten months.

"To Abraham he appeared as a traveler; to Joshua as a man of war. Christ will be to his people what their faith needs. Christ had his sword drawn, which encouraged Joshua to carry on the war with vigour. Christ's sword drawn in his hand, denotes how ready he is for the defence and salvation of his people. His sword turns every way. Joshua will know whether he is a friend or a foe . . . Joshua's inquiry shows an earnest desire to know the will of Christ, and a cheerful readiness and resolution to do it. All true Christians must fight under Christ's banner, and they will conquer by his presence and assistance.[134]

In this battle against the enemy, I was fighting under the banner of Christ. The victory would come because of His presence, because of the His defense.

Joshua had asked the commander of the Lord's army, "What message does my Lord have for his servant?" I began making a similar inquiry of the Lord each day. I looked at His reply to Joshua: "'Take off your sandals, for the place where you are standing is holy.' And Joshua did so."[135] In Old Testament times, taking off shoes was a sign of respect and submission to authority. I wanted to stand on holy ground; I wanted to obey my commander's orders; I wanted to be ready to face the immense, unconceivable task before me: an unknown future for our daughter and her husband, for our three grandchildren, and in turn, for ourselves. I wanted to demonstrate reverence and submission to my Lord; and like Joshua I earnestly desired to know the will of Christ and fight under His banner. I wanted Him to lead me. And I wanted to see victory in our battle: Victory over addiction, victory over fear, victory over the insurmountable.

I had inquired, "Lord, what message do you have for me, your servant?" Soon, I sensed a reply. I was to take off my sandals and stand on holy ground. Only then could be written of me," And *Kathi* did so."

On Sunday, the day before the sentencing, the kids spent the afternoon visiting their parents. Before they had to separate and say their goodbyes, from a distance, we observed Amber and Jesse seriously and gently talking to the children. Later, we learned that they were explaining that in the morning, they would likely be sentenced to jail. I was uncomfortable, knowing they were speaking about jail. I hated the word. But I had begun to trust our sweet Amber and renewed Jesse. I had begun to trust that as parents, they were working on behalf of their children. With anxious hearts we tucked the grandchildren into bed that night. With tender souls, our grandchildren prayed for their Mommy and Daddy and for the sentencing to take place the next day.

Monday, November 19 arrived. It was a most difficult day for us all. I wore my mother and father's wedding rings on a necklace chain around my neck. The rings lay close to my heart. I was glad my parents weren't physically there, to see and feel my pain, but so glad their rings were close to me. Their rings, once a symbol and a promise in their marriage, were now a symbol and a promise of their commitment and fidelity to me and to my family. It was a reassuring reminder of the heritage in Christ, which began in them and now continued in our family, finally including our once-wayward Amber and Jesse.

Ron drove the kids to school but didn't go on to work as usual. Instead, he came back home where we prayed and then drove to the courthouse. I was uneasy. I wanted to glorify God no matter the outcome. The courtroom was filled with family and friends. I felt blessed. Amber and Jesse sat at the front, waiting to be called up. But we waited quite a while. Others ahead of them received sentences. I grew frightened. We could tell the judge was giving harsh sentences for seemingly minor offenses. When persons went forward to be sentenced, their family members entered the courtroom. Some had family members. Some had none. But none of these persons had the support Amber and Jesse and Ron and I had. A young woman, crying, sat alone at the side of the courtroom. I went over, sat beside her, and put my arm around her, hoping to console her. She told me about her sister who would be arraigned on this day. Her short story was filled with hopelessness: a background of abuse and hate, a story of drugs, a child taken from her mother, no money for bail. I asked if I could pray for her and her sister. She allowed me to. Although I prayed for her sister by name, my prayer was for all women invaded by the enemies of abuse and neglect and deceived by the demons of drugs, for their crying and neglected children entwined in the lost cycle of it all. I had developed a greater empathy and sincere concern for persons in these situations. *Jesus Christ, we fight under your banner. Lead us.* The woman's sister, dressed in orange and white stripes, handcuffed, stood before the judge. The arraignment was stated. The officer led her from the courtroom. The young woman smiled a *thank you* through her tears as she left the courtroom. I returned to my seat and waited our turn.

I thought of the first time, nine months ago, I had entered this courthouse. I remembered seeing my daughter and her husband in shackles. I recalled the many court appearances speckled throughout the months between then and now, during which I had seen other women and men shuffling down the halls of the courthouse, in their faded striped coveralls, shackled hand and foot. Some hung their heads in shame; some were frightened; some smirked. No matter their demeanor, my heart had ached for each one; my hate for the deceitful enemy who had caused it all was refueled, but my awareness of the Father's great love for all and the saving grace of Jesus Christ was foremost in my thoughts. Now I looked at my daughter, her beauty and health returning to her once-addicted body. I observed my son-in-law, now a true man in every sense of the word, and I thanked God. They sat together knowing that most likely they would be separated for a lengthy time, and separated from their children as well. But they faced the consequences of their sins and crimes, thankful that God had saved them out of their depression and addiction, thankful that they had a bright future in Him.

The judge had stepped out and now reentered the courtroom. "All stand," the court assistant instructed.

Jesse was summoned first. His lawyer spoke. Then Jesse spoke, humbling himself before the court. The judge pronounced the sentence, "One year in the county jail." Jesse's face was enveloped in pain as the deputy court officer escorted him out. Our family cried. I hurt for Jesse, and I hurt for his children. A year without their daddy, even after he had become a good daddy. Amber tried to compose herself knowing she needed to stand before the judge next.

I knew it was difficult for Amber to stand and face the judge immediately after her Jesse had been taken to jail. I hadn't felt so helpless since her arrest nine months ago. There was not one thing I could do to change the course of events today. It seemed that it was all in the judge's hands, yet I knew it was truly in our Lord's hands. I trusted Him, and I trusted the judge.

Ron and I knew the judge. He and his wife had patronized our coffee shop. We believed him to be a godly man and we had committed this all to the Lord, even this sentencing. We had seen the miracle of God in transforming our Amber and Jesse. We knew we would see the mercy of God today. And although I trusted in God's mercy, it didn't change the pain I felt when Amber was sentenced.

Her lawyer spoke. Amber spoke, admitting her crime and regret, putting herself at the mercy of the court. "Ninety days in jail," the judge said. *Oh, no,* I thought, or spoke, or cried. I don't know which. I was numb. The deputy took Amber by the shoulder and began to escort her out of the courtroom. I rushed to the front, near the door where he was leading her, extending my arms to hug her one last time. "Get back," he shouted. "Don't touch her." Our eyes met—Amber's and mine. She was my daughter, my beautiful little baby girl.

Through clouded eyes I saw Ron crying and hugging our daughter Kristen, our son Matt, and Lynette. I was trying to make my way to them, but I couldn't seem to move. Our friends were talking. Some were smiling. I felt strange. Their lives would go on as usual after they left this courtroom, but ours wouldn't. I was broken. I had asked God for mercy, and we had received mercy. The drastically reduced sentences—from 76 years to one year or less—were evidences of His mercy shown through the wisdom of the judge. But the overwhelming pressures of the last nine months pressed in on me. All I could think of was, *How will we tell the children? How will we tell them their parents won't be with them for Christmas?* Emotionally crushed and physically weakened, I felt someone take my arm. My brother Larry had come to my rescue, as he had so many times throughout our childhood and the many years since. He helped me out of the courtroom and out of the building. The cool November air and warm sunshine stroked my face like a fresh touch from God. Ron and I drove straight home. Matt and Lynette and Kristen met us there. We regrouped and I once again knew the hope to which my Lord had called me. After a time of prayer and renewal, they headed home. Then Jake came and the three of us, as grandparents, went to the school to pick up the children and convey the bitter report.

The children were quiet. Perhaps they suspected to hear that their parents were in jail. Once they were all in the car collected from their three different schools, one of us, I don't remember which one, told them the sad news. Their parents had both been sent to jail. It was another one of those moments you never want to experience. Their faces were the saddest I had ever seen. I held back my tears. It was the least I could do for them. "Will they be with us for Christmas?" Kaylee asked.

"No, honey," I replied. I think those were the two most arduous words I'd ever spoken.

My sandals were off, and the place was holy. We knew the hope to which He had called us. Now we needed the healing he promised.

1. Hard pressed, perplexed, persecuted, struck down, feeling worthless, lost, hopeless, ruined. These are all conditions in which the enemy wants us to remain. Find contrasts to those conditions as you read the following passages and discover what God wants for you. Make notes of each discovery: Isaiah 41:8-13; 43:1-21; 44:1-5.

2. My prayer life changed as I recognized the tremendous love of my heavenly Father. Open conversation replaced lifelong struggles in prayer. When I was so hurt that I couldn't speak, His name became my prayer. At a loss for words, His Word became my prayer. Pause now and think about your relationship to God the Father in prayer. Ask Him to show you any wrong thoughts you have about prayer. Ask Him to help you to pray honestly, to teach you to pray. Then

listen to His answers. Prayer is as much listening as speaking. Write what He reveals to you.

3. Amber wrote a letter to meth. Not only was this action therapeutic, but it also spoke boldly to the demon that had shackled her for years. Are you shackled with an addiction or fear, with hate or resentment, with a grudge or a root of bitterness? Write a letter to the beast that is covering you. Then, with God's power, release this enemy, once and for all.

4. Read Isaiah 46:9-13. In the days leading up to the sentencing, some of the most trying days of my life, God used people in a variety of ways to minister to me. Read Isaiah 46:9-13. Consider how God has used "a bird" or "a man" or another means to bring about His plans for you. Write about it.

5. In the latter part of this chapter I shared that like Joshua I too began asking the Lord, "What message do you have for me, your servant?" We know that the Lord's response to Joshua was "Take off your sandals, for the place where you are standing is holy."[136] Review Joshua 3—5 leading up to Joshua's inquiry and the LORD's response (Joshua 5:13-15). I described above what "taking off my sandals" meant to me. What does "taking off your sandals" look like in your life? How will you step onto "holy ground?" As it was written about Joshua, "And Joshua did so," (Joshua 5:15b), how might it also be written of you, "And _____ did so"? (Write your name in the blank.) Write about it.

chapter seven

WHISPERS OF PROMISE
Trusting in His Every Word

*God's promises are sure. No matter how many
promises He has made, each one is more certain than the sunrise, more enduring than
the highest mountain, more abiding than the
deepest sea.*

~DAVID JEREMIAH

PROCESSING the PAIN

Heartache is hearing his sentence: One year in jail.

Heartache is watching your daughter suffer over the reading of his sentence.

Heartache is knowing that the children won't see their daddy for one year.

Heartache is hearing her sentence: Ninety days in jail.

Heartache is knowing that the children won't see their mommy for three months.

Heartache is seeing your beautiful daughter hand-cuffed and taken off to jail.

Heartache is not being able to hug her.

Heartache is knowing her dreams are on hold.

Heartache is carrying her cute green purse home to my closet.

Heartache is telling your grandchildren that their mom and dad were sent to jail.

Heartache is answering your grandchildren when they ask if Mom and Dad will be with them for Christmas. "No, honey."

And Jesus Whispered ~

Although the mountains around you are shaken, Kathi, and the hills are broken down, my unfailing love for you will not be shaken, nor will my promise of peace be removed. I am the Lord who has compassion for you and your precious grandchildren.

The grandchildren and Ron and I understood each other's pain on one level, a bond we shared only with their Poppy Jake and their aunts and uncles. As much as Ron and I had been hurt, we knew our position as adults was to be our children's comforters. No matter how we felt, we were responsible to meet our grandchildren's needs. It continued to be our primary goal.

Our relationship with these grandchildren was closer than typical as we had an understanding resulting from together suffering emotional pain that no child or parent was designed to bear. So on this evening after the sentencing, Ron and I held the children and tried to encourage them, "You know how much we all hurt nine months ago, when you were separated from Mom and Dad? We hurt so badly, we could barely stand it. But God helped us. You got to see your mom and dad. They were healed. Your family was happy again. Now, we are deeply hurt once more. But you will be happy again. It will be even better. And we will be right here loving you and helping you get through this temporary hurt. It won't be long before your mom will be out and you'll be with her. Then your dad will be out and your family will be all together again."

Papa and I both shared in tucking the kids into bed and saying their prayers with them. Every night, after they were sound asleep I tiptoed back into their bedrooms, knelt by their beds, and prayed, as I had done for the last nine months. I usually began with Benny, laying one hand on his head and my other hand on the bottom of his feet, praying *Father God, protect this child from the enemy. Keep him in your care from the top of his head to the tips of his toes. Command Your angels concerning Benny to guard him in all His ways. Comfort him and fill his heart with joy.* Then I crept to Jacob and Kaylee, kneeling, praying, and cherishing the quiet moments with them as well.

The evening of the sentencing was especially difficult for all of us. After the children were sound asleep and I had knelt by their beds and prayed, I checked them all through the night, whispering one word prayers: *Bless. Comfort. Touch. Heal.* Moving about our home throughout those unsettling nights, I felt the presence of the One who never sleeps nor slumbers.

And Jesus Whispered ~

I will never leave you, Kathi. I am watching over you day and night. The children are never out of my sight. You can rest in peace. While you rest, I will neither slumber nor sleep.

He had a plan I didn't know about. It was a plan to take everything that was "messed up" and work it all together for my good, for Ron's good, and for Amber and Jesse's good.

I Won't Be Receiving a Tony Award This year.

The date was set.
The courtroom was reserved.

The orchestration had already been assigned, and guess what?

I hadn't been chosen for the job.

I had wanted to do it; I had wanted to be able to arrange everything. To set the stage for the sentencing with the right people there and exactly the right words to be said. I had it all planned. I thought. But the orchestrator position belonged to someone else, Almighty God.

So I sat back and trusted God, something I've been learning to do for quite some time, trusting Him to orchestrate the events.

God began the orchestration quite some time ago, before the creation of the world. He created Amber's inmost being, her special talents, her tender soul. Then He knit her beautifully together, her delicate face, her porcelain complexion, her thin fingers, in my womb.

And while she was in my womb, I loved her. I planned how I would care for her, protect her, guide her, keep her. He had the same plans for her and more! Plans to prosper her and protect her, plans to give her hope and a future.

Time passed. I failed. She failed. We all failed Him.

I kept trying to orchestrate the events in her life. I kept applying for the position, but over and over, I was never hired.

I began to trust Him more. I learned to depend upon His Word.

I prayed that Word with her, to her, for her.

I kept asking the God of our LORD Jesus Christ, the glorious Father, to give us the Spirit of wisdom and revelation, so that we might know him better. I prayed that the eyes of our hearts might be enlightened in order that we might know the hope to which He has called us, the riches of His glorious inheritance, and His incomparably great power for us who believe.

And it happened. It seemed chaotic at first, like total discord, dissonance, cacophony. But the Great Orchestrator, the one who had written the composition, had arranged all the parts, and had adapted that beautiful composition to our broken lives. That Great Orchestrator, in His great mercy, brought all the parts of the production together in perfect harmony.

She was redeemed. She became a new creation.

And so each time I think the production is in shambles and needs orchestrated, I remind myself to quit applying for the position. There's someone more qualified, and He does such a perfect job.

No, I won't be receiving a Tony Award this year.

And Jesus Whispered ~

*I will bring about what I have promised you,
Kathi. What I have planned, that will I do.
I bring my righteousness to you. My salvation
will not be delayed. You can trust me.*

On Tuesday morning after a heartbreaking Monday, after telling our grandchildren that Mommy and Daddy were in jail, and after a miserable night, I opened my Bible to Joshua 5:14b to ask the Lord the question I had been trying to remember to ask Him every day, "What message, my Lord, do you have for me, your servant?" *Was I expecting something new on this Tuesday morning,* I wondered. *Something dramatic? Something unusual?* As I flipped through the pages of my Bible my eyes fell upon highlighted passages, sticky notes, and ink writings, smeared by time and wear. I read His promises. The same promises I'd been given in His Word before Monday's sentencing were true for me on Tuesday. The same God who loved us all before Monday's sentencing still loved us on Tuesday. Ron and I felt empty. But God was with us. Amber was hurting and lonely. But God was with her. Jesse was humiliated

and broken. But God was with him. God reminded me
that He promises He will never leave us or forsake us.[137]

And Jesus Whispered~

*Do you see, Kathi? I do not change. I am the
same yesterday, today, and forever. Let your
jar of clay hold all my treasures. Be healed,
my daughter. Be healed.*

SOAKING up the HEALING

I don't know exactly when the healing began. But
because of God's character we knew it came. Little by
little, we began to perceive it. Our home became a refuge
to the children, as it was to Ron and me. Along with three
vibrant grandchildren and a tired Nana and Papa living in
our home, we could sense the presence of Someone else. It
was the person of the Holy Spirit, permeating our home
and living within us. A passage in Romans in the Bible
told me that "the Spirit helps us in our weakness" (Romans
8:26). The word "helps" in this verse, means "takes hold
against."[138] The Holy Spirit was taking hold against in our

weakness. Imagine! The "Spirit himself" was interceding for us, "with groans that words cannot express" (Romans 8:26). As much as I had been groaning from the depths of my heart in the last nine months, the Holy Spirit was groaning more, interceding for us "in accordance with God's will" (Romans 8:26,27). Who could ask for more? Certainly the healing of our broken hearts was God's will. We all needed the comfort of the Heavenly Father.

Papa and Nana, Can I Lie in Your Bed?

He tends his flock like a shepherd: He gathers the lambs in his arms and carries them close to his heart (Isaiah 40:11).

I put her to bed, as usual. Well really with a bit more tenderness, a bit more time reading, laying, singing, snuggling. But she is still quite unsettled when I leave her bedside. Shortly after, I hear her ever so quietly entering our bedroom. "Papa and Nana, can I lie in your bed?"

"Sure, honey."

She steps up, up, up, onto the little white stepping stool and up, up, up, onto the big, soft mattress. And then I see the tears.

"I miss my mommy."

I wipe her tears.

I lie beside her my arm around her cherishing her soft hair on my cheek, breathing in her sweet, innocent scent.

Later, Papa carries sleeping Kaylee back to her own bed. I doze for a short time and then awaken in the night. My heart aches for my youngest daughter, Amber. I know some of the pain she is going through. She had shared with me months ago after the arrest. Now I know that she lies on her cot in her cell, cold and lonely. My throat makes a foreign noise. I try to hold back the sob, knowing that when it starts, it doesn't stop for a long time. I pray for her.

Months ago, after the arrest and before her recovery began, we brought Amber home on the 9th day, from that cell, from that cot, for one night in her own bed, her old bed, in the comfort of her old home, our home.

Now I want the comfort of my Papa's bed. I want that comfort for my daughter, and for her daughter, Kaylee. I want that comfort for Ron and for Jacob and Benny, and for all the hurting people I've seen these last nine months.

I find that comfort. I find it in the Word of God that is near me. Jesus reminds me of the comfort I have in Him.

And Jesus Whispered ~

I will tend to Kaylee. I will tend to Amber. I will tend to you, Kathi. I am your shepherd. I have gathered you in my arms, and I carry you close to my heart.

I met Karla at a conference that fall. A published author, pastor's wife, and mother of five, I immediately recognized Karla as a vibrant woman full of spark and creativity! I was quite surprised to learn of the struggles Karla was enduring: twin teenage boys with autism and an older son in prison for crimes resulting from drug use. In prison because of drugs. The words swirled in my mind as I compared her trauma to mine. My daughter and son-in-law had been sent to jail instead of prison, and sentenced for a short period of time rather than the original 76-year possibility.

While at the conference I noticed another woman who appeared to be quite the opposite of Karla. This little lady was sad looking, quiet, and kept to herself. I avoided her. I didn't want to meet her because I didn't want to hear about her troubles. *I'm going through such a sad time, myself, right now*, I thought. *I don't need to be burdened with other's problems.* At break times I met other people instead of her. At dinner I steered myself to other tables instead of hers. But the Lord nudged me one day and after that day's dinner I sat beside her and introduced myself. Then I began to listen, and I soon understood why her demeanor was so dismal. Her only son, the husband of a lovely young woman and father to two beautiful little daughters, had died of a drug overdose in an alley in Chicago, his lifeless body found next to a garbage can. Heroin was the demon. *Overdose. He died.* I hated the words. My daughter and son-in-law were alive and well. But it could have been them. They might have died from their drug use. Why was I spared the grief this woman had experienced? Why was I spared my daughter going to prison as Karla's son had?

And Jesus Whispered ~

There are so many things you do not know, Kathi. I love this woman as deeply as I love you. Give her my love as I have sent others to give you mine. Keep trusting Me. Your sons and daughters, grandsons, and granddaughters are taught by me and will have great peace. They are established in righteousness.

Believing, Therefore Speaking

Release joy like you release your faith, out of your mouth and from your heart.

Faith comes by hearing and hearing by the Word of God. It gets in your heart.

You release faith by saying. So what we say
has a lot to do with our joy.
~GLORIA COPELAND

Joy to the world; the Lord has come. Christmas was nearing, and with Amber and Jesse in jail, I didn't think joy to be possible. I visualized Ron and I holding and comforting sobbing children on Christmas Eve and Christmas day. But every day is God's day. So I set to listening for how God wanted us to do Christmas that year.

As a little girl, I loved Christmas. Sleigh bells rang in at night. Santa's sleigh tracks were found in the middle of the yard. Early Christmas morning my brother, sister, and I woke early, wrapped ourselves in warm bathrobes and quietly stepped down the big stairway to the living room where the brightly lit tree enveloped with cone-shaped electric bulbs of red, blue, green, orange, and white greeted us. Sleepy Mommy and Daddy met us by the tree and then made our day special. The true meaning of Christmas, the birth of Christ, was embedded in each fun tradition. Christmas was fun. And Christmas was joy.

As the young mother of little children, I also loved Christmas and wanted the celebration to be fun! On Christmas Eve, Ron read the Christmas story from his Bible. Matt, Kristen, and Amber slept in their warm flannels and footed sleepers, on the floor, their heads on pillows under the tree lights. They never heard Santa place the Detroit Lions football helmet, Cabbage Patch dolls, 4-wheeler Big Foot, or Care Bears under the tree, inches from their sweet, sleeping bodies. One Christmas, when Ron was out of work and the money was scarce, he made a 4-wheeler track for Matt and a horse stable for the girls. Christmas was fun. And Christmas was joy.

After our children were grown and had moved away, Christmas, although always joyous, was not as much fun anymore. Family gatherings, vital to the season, now had empty spots, once held by special grandpas, grandmas, aunts, or uncles. Songs and carols, once heard on the old, blonde 78-rpm player or later on the cassette tape, now brought a lump to my throat and an emptiness to my heart. Christmas was only as fun as I made it for the brief time the children came home. And Christmas was joy only when I allowed myself to find joy during those times.

But now, nearing the end of the most difficult year of my life, Bible readings reminded me that Paul tells us to rejoice in the Lord always.[139] He prayed for the Colossians to be strengthened with all might, according to God's glorious power, unto all patience and longsuffering with joyfulness.[140] Paul had suffered terribly, and yet he had discovered the secret to finding joy. It was being strengthened in God's power. I knew I needed to be strengthened. And I wanted joy. This concept found in the new covenant (testament) had been carried over from the old covenant (testament). "The joy of the LORD is your strength.[141] I wrote my commitment to finding that joy.

This Christmas season, I will find the joy that the Lord promises, and I will let it strengthen me.

I will find joy in remembering my Daddy and Mama and the legacy they left me.

I will find joy in the arms of my faithful husband.

I will find joy in my grown children who love and honor God.

I will find joy in my beautiful grandchildren. And I will find joy in a God who loves me and has granted me unmerited grace, increasing faith, and abundant hope through this year.

I will sing, "Joy to the world." And I'll find that joy when I sing, "The Lord is come."

I will "receive" my King.

I will "prepare Him room" in my heart, and I will fill that room with the joy He promises in His Word.

Joy to the world. The Lord is come.

Let Earth receive her King.
Let every heart prepare Him room,
and heaven and nature sing,
and heaven and nature sing,
and heaven and heaven and nature sing."

I sang with joy that Christmas season, and God strengthened me.

As the Lord had spared the children from numerous casualties in the past, His healing hand was still upon them. As each day went by, Ron and I could see their countenances brighten and their burdens lifted. The joy of Christmas filled them. I had foreseen this Christmas season as troublesome for us all, but I was wrong. The Counselor, the Holy Spirit, was teaching me that as Jesus had promised, He gave us peace.[142]

And Jesus Whispered ~

I don't create, want, or bring bad into your lives, Kathi. But I will take all those terrible events and work them for good for you and your loved ones because you love me. I have called you for a purpose. You can trust me. I promise.

My wonderful Jesus. I could trust Him to turn my sorrow into joy.

As surely and as quickly as I found joy in celebrating Christmas with the grandchildren, grief poked through the joy bubble, bringing sadness over this first Christmas without my father and mother. I had been missing them more lately and yearning to talk to them. Perhaps it was because of the holidays, or perhaps it was because I had been in their house quite often, sorting, cleaning, and getting it ready for new life. I was especially saddened that I no longer had them to impart confidence to me as they'd done all my life, the confidence of knowing they were praying for me and my family.

The Holy Spirit stirred me. Suddenly filled with joy, the Spirit reminded me that Daddy and Mama had spoken to the Lord Jesus many times on behalf of our entire family and me. I had witnessed those prayers numerous times through the years. The scene filled my mind. I crossed the yards toward their yellow house. As I neared the house I heard their tender voices crying out to the Lord for us, their family. I sometimes stood on the front porch and looked through the kitchen window, gazing on their wrinkled hands clutched together in prayer, resting on the kitchen table. And I recognized that those prayers were powerful and effective, and, offered in faith, they continued to rise as burning incense before the Father.[143] The Spirit comforted me through this pleasant reminder. And I thanked God for Daddy and Mama.

Even with the Lord's comfort, I had been suffering for some time. The Word told me to continue to find joy in that suffering.

"Through him we have gained access by faith into this grace in which we now stand. And we rejoice in the hope of the glory of God. Not only so, but we also rejoice in our sufferings, because we know that suffering produces perseverance; perseverance, character; and character, hope. And hope does not disappoint us, because God has poured out his love into our hearts by the Holy Spirit, whom he has given us."[144]

It was a difficult concept, the idea of rejoicing in our sufferings. I put it out there in a Bible study on my website, asking my readers, "If you are suffering, do you join me in wondering how in the world we can ever rejoice in suffering?"

I was overwhelmed by what God taught me through His Word and my study partners. I gleaned lessons in suffering and rejoicing from these honest ladies. One in particular conveyed this idea of joy in suffering and allowed me to share it with you. Amy is a mother of three boys and a girl, Halle, a vibrant 13-year-old. Halle was born with Hypoplastic Heart Syndrome, a congenital heart disease. She functions on a quarter of a normal heart. Halle has had many heart surgeries and procedures. And through the years Amy has seen many other children die with this disease. Recently, Amy wrote about one of Halle's visits to the pediatric heart specialist. I think, in reading between the lines, you can see the amazing outlook Amy and Halle both have in dealing with their suffering.

> I took Halle for her appointment. The report showed somewhat what I anticipated or thought was happening anyway. Her only ventricle is enlarged and slowing. The atrium tells it to beat and it says, *Uh, hmmm, what was it I was supposed to do?* Sometimes it listens immediately and responds; sometimes it's too tired. This explains the lower heart rate. However, it is still within the "acceptable" range for these type of heart patients, and her overall function is considered good. Her blood pressure was pretty high. The doc kept re-taking it and listening. After retaking it numerous times on all four limbs, they recorded it as high. He increased the dosage of two of her heart meds to help with function and hopefully slow down the "slow down" process. In other words, to keep her ventricle working for as long as we can on meds and to lessen the work load.

> While all of that is going on *with* that little heart of hers, much is going on *in* that little heart of

hers. On the way up to the hospital she was sharing how excited she was to be able to hand the doc $55.36, the money she had raised for heart families so far. She's all excited and vibrant about the whole thing and then innocently and excitedly says, "But really it wasn't me raising the money, it was all God. I mean, c'mon mom, what kid sells bracelets and raises that much?" (Yesterday our pastor gave a sermon about giving the glory to God. Halle wasn't there, didn't hear a word of it. It's something she naturally does.) *Lots going on in that heart of hers.*

Then, after that conversation we listened to the radio and she sang along to all the worship songs that came on, knowing the words to most of them. My mind did a flashback replay over our many trips. Before she could talk, she was humming worship music on our trips. Then it grew to, "Hoey is da woard, Gauwd awww-mighy." Now it's, "You are my King, Jesus. You are my King," clearly, precise, in tune, loudly, heartfelt—beautiful. *Lots going on in that heart of hers.*

Her regular doc was stranded in Lansing, so an older doc attended to her. This messed her plan up a bit because she really wanted to present the money to Dr. Russell. She wasn't sure what she to do, even asked me to decide for her or do it for her. I told her it was up to her. Doc Russell has known her since before she was born, so if she wanted to wait and give it to him that would be fine, but if she wanted to give it to this doctor I assured her that would be fine as well. The doctor was closing it up, saying someone would be in to hook up her halter, when Halle walked forward and gave him the money. She explained she was selling bracelets to raise money for heart research and families and this was the money she had raised so far. She said, "And this is for you," as she tied one of the bracelets she had made around his wrist. This older doc is one who has been around since the first hypoplast patient. One who has most likely seen way too many deaths. One who has been fighting for these heart kids for many, many years and has seen most of them born, live, and die. This older doc, got teary eyed as she tied that bracelet around his wrist. *Lots going on in that heart of hers.* I'm human. These days exhaust me like no other. Halle comes back still vibrant and full of energy, and I come back feeling like a tractor flipped on me and dragged me a few hundred feet. I have a choice, choosing to focus on what's going on *in* that heart of hers, rather than *with* that heart of hers. My job has always been simple. Love her. Got that down. I love, live, laugh, and pray.

Responding to the idea of rejoicing in suffering, Amy wrote,

It really is *joy.* Is it the happy, skipping, life is wonderful, kind of joy? No. But it is the incredible joy of having that intimate, deep, dependence on, and relationship with God. When nothing makes sense, when all is dark, when all seems lost, that's when His light of peace and *joy* penetrate your soul. Yes indeed, there is joy in suffering. The wonderful, incredible joy of holding hands, and being held by our great, loving, compassionate Father."

I gained a greater understanding of suffering through Amy's testimony. *So the joy isn't in suffering; the joy is in having Him so near.*

And nothing spoke to me as powerfully as the Word of God I quoted earlier. It reveals the end result of suffering, from suffering to perseverance; from perseverance to character; and from character to hope. The end result is hope.

> *True faith means holding nothing back. It means putting every hope in God's fidelity to His Promises.*
> ~Francis Chan

Hope is expectation, expecting that God's promises are true. Faith is confidence in that expectation and assurance even when we can't see it. Our journey with Amber had taught us to have faith and expectation in the God who loved us so.

And Jesus Whispered ~

You will never be disappointed when you place your hope in me, Kathi, because your

Father God has poured out His love into your heart by the Holy Spirit, whom He has given you.

We counted on God's promises and I cherished each one, but when my mind became cluttered with obstacles, I couldn't always remember the promises. Months before I had written promises on lined paper, every promise I found in the Bible. I needed to see the promises and speak the promises. So I relied upon that list, locating them in the Bible and speaking them for myself, for Ron, for Amber and Jesse, and for each one in our family. The power of life and death is in the tongue,[145] including my tongue, and I had decided to peak life. I wrote and spoke and prayed and praised Him for His promises. Here are a few of the promises turned into my prayers.

I have received a precious faith. Your divine power has given me great and precious promises.[146]
You have promised me so much, Lord. You promised me that if I raised my child in the way she should go, she would not turn from it, and Lord, she is now a new creation in you.[147]

I asked for it, Lord because you had told me that you will do whatever I ask in your name to bring glory to the Father, and you granted it.[148]

I remind myself that your promises are true now and forever, true for me and for Ron and for Amber and Jesse. I can count on your promises now and I do count on your promises now.[149]

My desire ends only in good.[150]

The judge's wisdom gives him patience; it is to his glory to overlook an offense.[151]

My humility and righteous fear of you, O God, the Father, brings wealth and honor and life. It brings children who are honoring you—grandchildren who have life with their parents.[152]

I pursue righteousness and love. I will find life, prosperity, and honor.[153]

There is a future for me; my hope will not be cut off.[154]
I am (we are) blessed. My children will be mighty in the land. We will continue to be blessed. Wealth and riches are in my house; my righteousness endures forever. Even during this time of "apparent" darkness, light dawns for us because you, O Lord, are a gracious, compassionate, and righteous man. Good will come to us; I have no fear of bad news. My heart is steadfast; I trust in you, Lord . My heart is secure; I have no fear; in the end, I will look with triumph on my foes. My dignity is lifted high in honor.[155]

Show us your strength O God, as you have done before. Summon your power, O God. Rebuke the beast.[156]

Because I have clean hands and a pure heart, I will receive your blessing—and my generation is such, Matt, Kristen, Amber, and their families.[157]

I trust in you. You will not let me be put to shame; my enemies will not triumph over me. Remember your great mercy and love. Do not remember my sin or Amber and Jesse's sin. For the sake of your name, forgive our iniquity, though it is great. (I know you have.) I will spend my days in prosperity and my children will inherit the land. Redeem us, O God, from all our troubles.[158]

Your joy, O Lord is my strength.[159]

Because I obey you, Lord, I will be blessed wherever I am and my children, Matt, Kristen, and Amber, will be blessed all the time.[160]

Because I obey your commands, you will send refreshing rain to bless us . . . we will be satisfied. (Oh, how I look forward to that rain.)[161]

No longer will Jacob be ashamed; they will keep your name Holy and will stand in awe of you. Let Amber and Jesse live in peaceful dwelling places, in secure homes, in undisturbed places of rest; how blessed they will be. You tend us like a shepherd; you gather us in your arms and carry us close to your heart. You gently lead us with our young (Jacob, Ben, Kaylee).[162]

We had celebrated an early Christmas get-together with our entire family. Christmas Eve and day were special times for Ron and me and the grandchildren. Both parents had recorded their voices on special audio books. The children opened these books on Christmas Eve. Then their mommy and daddy each phoned them on Christmas morning. The grandchildren had received gifts from mommy and daddy, as well as gifts from Papa and me. We had a nice day together, celebrating Christ's birth and enjoying presents. Later in the day, they went to Poppy's and celebrated with more family.

Amber phoned us again and explained her Christmas day behind bars. Like me, she had assumed that Christmas day would be extremely difficult for her; but she turned it around and decided to find joy in the midst by truly celebrating Jesus' birth. She gathered all the women inmates together and led them in a discussion of Christmas and in prayer. It was a blessed time for her and for many of the women. I know it brought glory to God.

Christmas Day was over. I enjoyed having the grandkids home from school during the next week of their Christmas break. The New Year came, and as I wondered what it would bring for us, I heard promises from Jesus.

And Jesus Whispered ~

I know the plans I have for you. My plans are to prosper you and not to harm you or yours. My plans are to give you hope and a future. Call to me anytime, my beloved, and I will be found by you. I will bring you back. I will answer you and show you great and mighty things which you do not yet know.

I responded to His whisper in prayer., *I will call and I will find You. You will bring me back and answer. You will show me! Thank you for your promises.*

I missed my precious daughter while she was incarcerated. For the first time in many years she was open, loving, caring, and concerned. How I wanted to experience my new Amber. I yearned to hug her and be hugged by her. To feel the touch of her cheek on mine. To give counsel and to receive her counsel. I wanted to talk to her about the children. These things could not take place at this time, but behind the bars, she spent much time praying and contemplating her new life in Christ. She made the most of God's plan for her at this time.

Although we saw other children of inmates at the jail visitations, she and Jesse and DHS decided that the children would not visit them during their incarceration. I had mixed feelings about it but in their circumstances it turned out to be best. Ron and I visited her at every opportunity, which was usually on Saturday mornings. Times were bittersweet.

Nothing Can Separate the Love of a Mother and Her Daughter

Do not park in the front drive.

Do not take anything into the visiting room.

Sit at all times.

Do not touch the glass.

And so we sit, the glass between us. Our hands pressing, hers on one side, mine on the other. And I can imagine the touch of her soft skin as if I were holding her hand, as if there were no glass between us.

We talk through a phone. We speak of love and forgiveness. We speak of redemption. We speak of a future.
It reminds me of the love of God. The love that takes the things in our lives, even the bad, and works those things for the good of us who love him.

We rejoice together because, you see, nothing can separate the love of a mother and her daughter.

I leave, for now. Saddened by our present circumstances but rejoicing in the nearness of God.

"Who shall separate us from the love of Christ? Shall trouble . . . . No, in all these things we are more than conquerors through him who loved us. For I am convinced that neither death nor life, neither angels nor demons, neither the present nor the future, nor any powers, neither height nor depth, nor anything else in all creation, will be able to separate us from the love of God that is in Christ Jesus our Lord."[163]

The New Year brought busy days once again, with a return to our routines and a new semester for the kids. Soon, with the reward of an early release, it was time for Amber to be released from incarceration. I wrote about this exciting time.

Tomorrow at Midnight

Tomorrow, at midnight, her daddy will be at the back door of the building.
Tomorrow, at midnight, her daddy will pick her up, his precious daughter, his youngest daughter.

She's coming home to her new life—free of the addiction, the guilt, and the darkness of the past.

She's coming home to her children, her beautiful children who have weathered the storm and are awaiting the comfort of their mommy's arms. They await the sound of her voice, the coconut fragrance of her hair, and the touch of her fingers stroking the nape of their necks as she sings them to sleep.

She's coming home to her new home a big yellow house bathed in love and steeped in tradition and heritage.
Her recovery is complete; her debt is paid; her punishment is over.

She will step out and breathe in the cold, crisp, fresh air.

And she'll thank God for the new life He has given her.

And tomorrow at midnight, I'll thank God again, as I promised Him last year, and will forever and ever, for the new life in Christ He gave my precious daughter, my youngest daughter.

Upon her release, Amber would be on probation and closely monitored by the court. Although it made sense to us that she would live in our home with us and the children, the court did not allow this. DHS still had control over the situation. They did not yet permit her to have the children living with her. She needed a home in which to live, and she had one. My parents' yellow house next door. It had been the home of my mother and father for nearly 60 years, and as I wrote earlier, it was bathed in love and steeped in tradition and heritage. We could sense the presence of the Holy Spirit in the yellow house. We had updated the house and made needed improvements.

Now it was ready to serve as home to someone special. My siblings and I welcomed Amber to occupy the home until it could be sold.

Ron picked Amber up at 12:01 am on her release date. He brought her to our house where she stepped into the kids' bedrooms and kissed each one in their sleep. It was sweet. I offered to sleep with her at her house, the yellow house next door, but she preferred to be alone that night.

Early the next morning, she drove to the courthouse where she met with her probation officer. Rules, regulations, and stipulations were placed upon her. She was to attend addiction counseling, meet with the probation officer, complete regular and random drug tests, and pursue employment. DHS limited her time with the children. They arranged for transition counselors to regularly meet with Amber and the children. Supposedly they were working toward returning the children to Amber's care. We had expected Amber to be elated with her newfound freedom, but, instead, she was overwhelmed and suddenly seemed depressed. Within a few days, she drove herself to the Kalamazoo Gospel Mission, where she met with the counselor who had advised Amber during her nine months in the program. Later that day, she came home a different person—again filled with joy! God was so good.

Throughout the next months, DHS placed the children with Amber for short stays, which increased weekly. The transition counselors literally sat in the house with Amber and the children while they ate meals and while Amber assisted the children with their homework. Amber had difficulty handling the situation gracefully, but she had learned to not only cope, but also to work with people and take responsibility for her own actions. It helped to know that these people really were working on behalf of the children and Amber. In time, Amber proved herself to DHS as much as they would trust her at the time. Nonetheless, DHS still wanted control over the children.

Three months after her release from jail we attended another hearing at Probate Court. Again the court would decide upon a continuing plan for the children. DHS asked for another three months of control. The children's court-appointed attorney spoke in their behalf. "Mrs. Modert does not need to learn to parent her children," he said. "She needs to stay clean. I feel it is in the best interest of the children to have a sense of normalcy returned to their lives and to live with their mother full time." The judge ordered that the children would no longer be under DHS jurisdiction but would be completely reunited with their mother! What a joyous day it was for us all, especially for our beautiful daughter, Amber! Ron and I helped the children get settled in their home with their mother. The yellow house next door. The home steeped in love and heritage. God was so good!

Promises Fulfilled

This Nana Has No Regrets. Only Precious Memories

I awoke this morning to an empty house. Empty and quiet. No little girl stood beside my bed, looking at me and asking the usual Saturday questions: "Where's Papa? Can we get up, Nana? I'm not sleepy anymore."

I made only one bed—mine. Jacob, Ben, and Kaylee's beds had not been slept in.

I went to my kitchen and watched the *Morning Show* instead of Saturday morning cartoons. I leisurely drank coffee and fixed my own breakfast instead of Kaylee's. Then I wrote my grocery list and found it to be short.

I feel strange and somewhat lonely. The house is not the same.

I'm remembering the last 14 months. The house has been filled with dolls and Legos, backpacks and half-eaten granola bars. I've rescued socks from between the sheets and I've sorted outfits for each day of the week. The fridge held large jugs of Powerade® and organic 2% milk; the pantry had been packed with Honey Nut Cheerios® and Salt and Vinegar Potato Chips; and the freezer had been stocked with Cookie Dough ice cream. Laundry room hooks held fleece jackets and hoodies; its shelves had been stacked with boots, shoes, and baseball cleats; and its hampers overflowed with dirty jeans and white t-shirts. Crumbs had covered the floors under the kitchen stools; Happy Meal® trinkets had bounced from one room to another; and blobs of blue toothpaste had enthusiastically splattered the bathroom counters.

This Nana took on the traits of Mommy. (It's an awesome combination.) And Papa added the role of Daddy to his character. (It's a huge responsibility.)

The savings account dwindled. The vehicles' odometers soared as the road less traveled became the road more traveled.

Evenings had been filled with baseball games, homework and baths, snuggling and lullabies. Weekends meant wrestling meets, visiting Mommy and Daddy, and going to church.

Nana and Papa forgot that they once went out to dinner, sat quietly and talked, and watched old movies on television.

I had given some last minute instructions to the children:

"Kaylee, here are your little pink washcloths. I'm packing them for you to take."

"Benny, don't forget to brush your teeth morning and night."
"Jacob, your baseball uniform is washed and ready for your first game next week."

I'm remembering the last 14 months, when this house has been a refuge and a haven of unconditional love to three adorable grandchildren. This Nana has no regrets. Only precious memories.

The day Jacob and Ben and Kaylee have been waiting for has finally come. They are home with their mommy. Home where they belong. And waiting for their daddy.

I couldn't be happier. But it is somewhat bittersweet, and . . .

I feel strange and lonely in this empty, quiet house. The house is not the same.

Proverbs 22:6 promises us that if we "Train a child in the way he should go, when he is old, he will not turn from it". How many thousands of parents have prayed that verse through the years. And how many times have parents become discouraged because they don't see that prayer being answered. But we must remember that whatever we ask, according to God's will, will be given. We know it is God's will that our children love and honor Him, so we must never, ever give up praying and believing.

I studied and contemplated God's will for my children and grandchildren. Among many passages, I considered the powerful, promising words found in Isaiah 49:25b, "And your children I will save".

I might not know God's will about my job, about which car to drive, about whether or not to replace the carpeting in my living room. But I do know His will regarding my children. The Bible is filled with promises about my children, so many that as I read them, I list them and often return to the list. I remind myself of God's desires. I know it is God's will that my children honor Him. I know it is God's will that my children are taught by the Lord, that they are established in righteousness, and that they continue the heritage of His Kingdom. I know it is God's will that they are blessed by Him, that they have plenty, and that they have a secure fortress and refuge in the Lord. I know it is God's will that my children have great peace. He tells me to pray. And so I continue to pray.

You see, this is their heritage. And we, as parents, shall never, ever give up praying for their heritage.

The new Amber began raising her children in the yellow house, the one steeped in love and heritage, and she continues to live there today. Within a short time, she obtained employment, not through employment agencies to which she went regularly as she was required to do, but through a Christian acquaintance. I was reminded of God's promise to fulfill His purpose in Amber's life, "My purpose will stand, and I will do all that I please . . . to fulfill my purpose. . . I am bringing my righteousness near. It is not far away; my salvation will not be delayed."[164] Amber's employment became not simply a job, but a job she still enjoys, with good pay, hours that coordinated with her children's schedules, an outlook for advancement, and a gracious, Christian employer who provides perks and benefits.

The children finished the school year, adjusted to their new home, and enjoyed the presence of their mother. Amber and the children joined us in our family vacation at Maranatha that summer. They were happy but incomplete. Little Kaylee often reminded me that their family would not be complete until their daddy was with them. After seven months of incarceration, Jesse was granted work release four days a week to work with his dad in the lawn care business. It was a blessing, both emotionally and financially, as he was able to use the income to pay his financial debt owed to the county accumulated by incarceration. That daily work release also enabled him to have an easier adjustment to his later full time release from jail. As the time of Jesse's release neared, some non-violent prisoners were released early due to over-crowding. We were hoping Jesse would be one of these, but he was not. We didn't know why until the day of his release finally came. Jesse's cellmate was a hardened criminal, filled with hate and anger. He had often been heard raging threats against those who had sent him to jail, including the judge and his children. In revenge, had vowed to get the judge's children addicted to drugs. Throughout his incarceration Jesse had been a witness of Christ's love to the other inmates. On the evening before his release Jesse led his vile cellmate to the Savior, the One who is not willing that any should perish. Now we understood why Jesse hadn't been granted an earlier release. It was a part of God's plan for Jesse and for his cellmate.

And Jesus Whispered ~

Kathi, what I have told you in the dark, you must now speak in the daylight; the things I've whispered in your ear, you must now proclaim from the roofs.

As I write this closing chapter, over five years have passed since that unwanted phone call in the night, between that normal Tuesday and that wretched Wednesday. Amber and Jesse have remained upstanding, responsible citizens; caring, diligent parents; and remarkably transformed servants of God. They are actively serving in their church, volunteering at the Celebrate Recovery program at the jail, ministering to the lost, and speaking to groups of hundreds about their changed lives through the grace and mercy of God.

One day I shared their awesome testimony with a Christian I knew. He was amazed, yet responded, "They will have to fight that addiction now for the rest of their lives." Baffled, but not set back by his response, I replied, "No! They've been delivered from that addiction by the mighty power of God. They've been healed." Certainly both Amber and Jesse will battle temptation as any of us do, but we don't believe what the world says about their futures. Instead, we believe the Word—God's Word. His promises are fulfilled.

Jacob, Ben, and Kaylee are growing, healthy and strong. Jacob is in college. All three are active in sports and school activities, enjoy their friends, and are flourishing in their relationships to the LORD who spared them from the world's expectations of children of drug users. We didn't believe what the world said about their futures. Instead, we believed the Word—God's Word. His promises were fulfilled.

1. When you have experienced deep heartache, how did you process the pain? How did you adjust to the reality of what must be, even if it would only be temporary?

2. Read John 10:10. Who brings bad things into our lives? Who brings good into our lives?

Now read Romans 8:28. What does God promise to do with the bad things the thief, our enemy, Satan, brings into our lives?

3. Read Romans 5:1-5. Consider the word, rejoice. What does it mean? Use a Bible concordance such as that on Biblegateway.com to find other verses or passages that include the Word rejoice or joy. Let each verse teach you a bit of what it means to rejoice. Narrow your findings to those verses or passages that help explain the connection found in rejoicing and suffering. In your own words, write what the Bible tells you about rejoicing (or joy) and suffering.

4. A segment in this last chapter was titled "Believing, Therefore Speaking." In my journey of believing the Word of God, I learned the importance of speaking the Word. Read Proverbs 18:21. As I wrote earlier, "The power of life and death is in the tongue, including my tongue, and I had decided to speak life." I spoke joy instead of sadness during the Christmas season. I spoke life about and over my grandchildren. I also began to understand the danger of speaking words the enemy could use against me, knowing that

my words had the power of death, as well as the power of life. Ask the Lord to show you negative statements or connotations you speak. And if you falter, don't fret! Just rebuke the enemy and change that negative statement into a positive one, all in the name of Jesus.

5. Read Titus 1:2, "in hope of eternal life, which God, who cannot lie, promised before time began". What attribute of God is revealed in this verse? How does this knowledge and confidence speak to you?

6. Which of God's promises have you depended upon? If you can remember a word or two but not the location of the verse use your Bible concordance and look up those words. List some below.

As you study the Bible, consider keeping a notebook or journal in which you list His promises. As you note them, speak, pray, and praise God for each.

Go Back . . . and when you get there

After Elijah began listening to the Lord's gentle whisper, had some rest and food, had made his excuses before the Lord, and had admitted his fears, the Lord said, "Go back the way you came . . . When you get there, anoint Hazael . . . Jehu . . . and Elisha."[165] The Lord God had been patient and loving with Elijah. Elijah's work was not finished. He was to anoint kings and was to anoint Elisha as a prophet to succeed him. The Lord God also has plans for you, and for me, as well. My work is not done. I am to teach, to serve, and to lead others to receive the anointing of the Lord. Ask Him what He wants you to do.

Jesus was teaching, healing, and preaching, when John the Baptist sent his disciples to ask Him, "Are you the one . . . or should we expect someone else?" [166]

Jesus replied, "Go back and report . . . what you hear and see: The blind receive sight, the lame walk, those who have leprosy are cured, the deaf hear, the dead are raised, and the good news is preached to the poor. Blessed is the man who does not fall away on account of me."[167] I ponder this scene in my mind. They come to Jesus to inquire if He is the one they've been expecting? You see, they knew the Messiah was coming. They had been awaiting the fulfillment of the prophecy for a long time. But they didn't know if this Jesus was the one.

I contemplate how I will respond to Jesus' statement, "Go back and report . . . what you hear and see."[168]

I hear the phone ringing in the middle of the night. I hear a message, a message I don't want to hear. I see my daughter and her husband in shackles, a sight I don't want to see.

I hear God's comforting voice, speaking to me in my deepest pain. I see his angels surrounding me. I feel His tender arms holding me, lifting me up when I feel I can't go on. I experience His amazing grace and His unfailing love that pulls me through the agonizing moments of each day.

I see a miracle. The dreaded message of that dark night yields to the Light of the World. He removes the shackles of bondage and addiction forever. He transforms my daughter and her husband by the power of the resurrected Christ. He equips them as they continue to give their lives to the Lord Jesus, the God of miracles.

I hear my daughter and her husband speaking of God, who they know personally. Telling of His amazing, saving grace. I see their changed lives. I see the light at the end of the tunnel. I see a bright and promising future. I see a new love and a new life. I see a couple nurturing their wounded children in a beloved yellow house, parenting them, loving them, and guiding them in the love of the Lord.

How might you respond to Jesus' statement, "Go back and report . . . what you hear and see"?

What if I HaveNothing Good to Report

Perhaps at this time, you are relating to only the first part of my response—hearing things you don't want to hear and seeing things you don't want to see. You haven't yet heard the good report you've been waiting for, or you haven't yet seen that miracle for which your heart yearns. Maybe you sit beside your loved one and wonder why the healing hasn't yet come. It may be that your heart breaks over the rejection of one you so deeply love. Possibly you visit your loved one behind bars or you observe his or her broken life from afar, feeling every puncture and wound your loved one receives as though it were inflicted upon your own body. Emptiness fills your days and at night your head lies on a tear-drenched pillow. Your knees ache from hours of prayer and your throat is swollen from uncontrollable sobbing. You wonder *if* or *when* your prayers will be answered, *if* God is listening, *if* He cares.

When Jesus walked amongst us, He told us that in this world we will have many trials and sorrows. It's not a pleasant message for us. It's one we don't like to hear, and I'm sure one that broke His heart as he spoke it, knowing how difficult these trials and sorrows would be for us. But our Savior didn't leave us without hope. He encouraged us that we can have peace in Him because He has overcome this world (John 16:33 NLT). That peace comes when we *listen* to Him, to His whispers, the whispers found in His Word. Listening, we can rest in Him. I know. I know because He continues to whisper to me, most often through His Word. Listening to those whispers, I am reminded that I can rest in Him.

Trials and sorrows didn't cease in my life when the healing came for my daughter, Amber, and her family. Other trials and sorrows, different but as vast and painful, are present today, striking me and my family, relentlessly gnawing away at my peace, trying to rob me of my rest in Jesus. I must constantly listen.

And Jesus Whispered ~

I am with you until the end of the ages, Kathi. I give you my peace. It's not the kind of peace the world gives or understands. It's of the covenant, the promise I spoke of. Let my Holy Spirit remind you of everything I have whispered to you in the past. Take my peace, my daughter. It's yours. Rest in it.

My heart is renewed as I listen to his whispers. I gratefully accept His offer of peace as I remember His faithfulness to me, and I encourage you, as well. Don't lose heart, my friend. Don't give up. Let your spirit be renewed each day (2 Corinthians 4:16 NLT). He hears you; He weeps with you; He cares. You are His child. Listen for His whispers. Let Him speak to you in your deepest pain. It is only through listening that we can find rest. As you rest, contemplate your response to Jesus' statement, "Go back and report . . . what you hear and see." I think you will hear and see His faithfulness in every trial and in every sorrow.

They asked Jesus, "Are you the one?"[169]

Yes, my friend, Jesus is the one. He is the Jesus of miracles, the one who heals the sick and broken hearted, the one who mends broken families. He is the one sent by God the Father to redeem you. He is the one who loves you. I encourage you to trust Him, to obey His Word, to never give up believing that He will deliver and heal you and your loved ones that He will give you His peace and that you find will rest in Him. I pray that *When Life Roars*, you'll hear *Jesus Whisper*.

God has changed my life forever. The façade of perfection is gone. In its place is the truth of brokenness and redemption, of light in the darkness. My heart is now more compassionate for those who are broken and cheated by the enemy; for those in shackles, concrete or abstract; for those who are sick and afflicted; and for those who are lost. My heart and lips now pray for them and my arms reach to care for them. I pray for truth to be revealed and grace to be granted, for faith to be increased and mercy to be extended, for comfort to meet sorrow and hope to be known. And I pray for the promises of God to be revealed in their lives. I know it's not too much to ask of our God. After all, He is trustworthy in all He promises and is faithful in all He does.[170]

About the Author

Kathi Waligora is an inspiration-al speaker, having spoken to Christian Women's Clubs, retreat conferences, and ladies' events, sharing her testi-mony and messages from God's Word. She has a B.A. from Olivet College and an M.A. from Spring Arbor Universi-ty. She has taught English at both sec-ondary and college levels. Addition-ally, Kathi is a business entrepreneur, restoring an 1879 Victorian building  and running a successful restaurant/retail establishment, along with her husband, in southern Michigan for several years.

Kathi is passionate about her ministry at Tommy's House, a recovery/transition home in Michigan, where she supports and encourages women recovering from addiction.

Married for forty-six years, Kathi and her husband, Ron, are the parents of three grown, married children and are Nana and Papa to eleven of Michigan's sweetest kids. They live in wooded surroundings in southern Michigan throughout three seasons and tropical surroundings in southern Florida during the winter.

Kathi maintains a blog on her website, reaches thousands through her writer's page on social media, and enjoys corre-spondence with a multitude of readers. She delights in weaving her own experiences with grace, grief, and family into her writing. Her compassion for others, a result of those person-al experiences, brings comfort and hope to her readers and audiences. To read more of Kathi's writing, visit her website at www.kathiwaligora.com and her Facebook Writer's page: www.facebook.com/KathiWaligoraChristianWriterSpeaker/. Kathi can be contacted for speaking engagements through her Face-book writer's page or through email: kathiwaligora@gmail.

Notes

1 https://www.goodreads.com/quotes/113822-night-is-a-time-of-rigor-but-also-of-mercy

2 John 8:12 NIV

3 John 10:10 NIV

4 Matt. 13:25, 27, 28, 38, 39 NIV

5 Ephesians 6:10-13 NIV

6 Ephesians 6:14 NIV

7 Ephesians 4:15 NIV

8 Ephesians 6:14b-16 NIV

9 Ephesians 6:17 NIV

10 Romans 10:17 NIV

11 Psalm 91:14-15 NIV paraphrased

12 Hebrews 4:12 NIV

13 Psalm 29:2,4 NIV paraphrased

14 Psalm 30:1-3 NIV paraphrased

15 Psalm 31:1-19 NIV paraphrased

16 1 John 3:9 NIV

17 1 John 4:4 NIV paraphrased

18 Matthew 12:28 NIV paraphrased

19 1 John 1:9-10,NIV

20 Hebrews 7:12 NIV

21 Isaiah 45:18-19 NIV

22 Ephesians 6:13 NIV

23 Ephesians 6:14 NIV

24 Ephesians 4:15 NIV

25 Colossians 1:4,5 NLT

26 Colossians 1:5,6 NIV

27 2 Corinthians 12:9 KJV

28 Titus 2: 11, 12 NIV

29 1 Kings 19:10, 14 NIV

30 Romans 5:17 NIV

31 Exodus 3:12 NASB
32 Hebrews 10:23 NIV
33 Romans 10:17 KJV
34 Psalm 24:4 NIV
35 Ephesians 6:12 NIV
36 Matthew 18:20 NIV
37 John 13:14 NIV
38 John 15:7 NIV
39 1 John 5:14, 15 NIV
40 Ephesians 6: 13-17 NIV
41 Psalm 57:10 NIV
42 Psalm 85:10 NIV
43 Psalm 85:11 NIV
44 Psalm 117:2 NIV
45 Lamentations 3:23 NIV
46 Psalm 89:14 NIV
47 Psalm 139:5 NIV
48 Ephesians 6:16 NIV
49 Matthew 17:20 NIV
50 2 Chronicles 20:15-17 NIV
51 Romans 10:8 NIV
52 1 King 19:9, 13 NIV
53 Thomas L. Constable, "Notes on 1 King," Dr. Constable's Expository (Bible Study) Notes, 2017 Edition, soniclight/constable/notes.htm
54 1 Kings 19:15, 16 NIV
55 Exodus 19:16-18; 1 Kings 18:38, 45
56 1 Kings 19:11,12 NIV
57 1 Kings 19:12 NIV
58 1 Kings 19:13 NIV
59 1 Peter 5:7 NLT
60 Romans 10:17 NIV
61 Psalm 141:3 NIV

62 Ephesians 1:18 NIV

63 Romans 9:23 NIV

64 Romans 9:25 NIV

65 2 Corinthians 5:21 NIV

66 Ephesians 2:8,9 NIV

67 1 Corinthians 11:24,25 NIV

68 Genesis 1:1-5 NIV

69 Ephesians 5:14 NIV

70 Ephesians 4:17-5:2 NIV

71 1 Kings 19:18 NIV

72 Romans 12:5 HCSB

73 Ephesians 4:12 HCSB

74 Romans 9:15 NIV

75 Psalm 34:8 NLT

76 "Salvation," http://www.josephprince.org/daily-grace/salvation/

77 http://www1.cbn.com/music/matt-redman-your-grace-finds-me

78 1 Kings 19:5 NIV

79 1 Kings 19:7 NIV

80 "Elijah Under the Broom Tree," https://godasagardener.com/2012/04/15/elijah-under-the-broom-tree/comment-page-2/

81 1 Kings 19:1-9a NIV

82 1 Kings 19:7 NIV

83 1 Thess. 4:13-18

84 John 11:33-36 NIV

85 Based on John 11:43

86 Psalm 112:4 NIV

87 Lamentations 3:22, 23 NIV

88 Psalm 73:23-26 NIV

89 Psalm 112:4 NIV

90 Matthew 5:4 NASB

91 Kent, Carol, *When I Lay My Isaac Down*, Navpress, 2004. 175-176

92 Romans 8:28 NIV

93 Exodus 20:221 NIV

94 Based on Hebrews 13:5b NIV

95 Deuteronomy 34:8 NIV

96 Isaiah 61:3 NIV

97 Isaiah 40:6-8 NIV

98 Habakkuk 3:3b, 4 NIV

99 2 Peter 1:4 NIV

100 Proverbs 6:20-23 paraphrased

101 Genesis 1:4 NIV

102 Psalm 3:1,2 NIV paraphrased

103 Psalm 68:28 NIV

104 Psalm 107:16, 20 NIV araphrased

105 Acts 10:38 NIV

106 Acts 1:8 NIV

107 1 John 2:20 NIV

108 2 Corinthians 8:12 NIV

109 Romans 5:1, 2 NIV

110 Romans 8:37 NIV paraphrased

111 2 Corinthians 4:7 NIV

112 2 Corinthians 4:7 NKJV paraphrased

113 Psalm 119:11 NIV paraphrased

114 Hebrews 13:8 NIV

115 Isaiah 52:2 NIV brackets mine

116 Isaiah 52:7 -12 NIV paraphrased

117 Ephesians 1:17 NIV

118 Ephesians 1:17 NIV

119 Ephesians 1:18 NIV

120 from Ephesians 6:16 NIV

121 Psalm 68:28, 30 NIV

122 Isaiah 54:13-17, NIV paraphrased

123 Psalm 68:28, 30 NIV

124 Psalm 5:11-12 NIV

125 Matthew 4:10 NIV

126 Matthew 16:23 NIV

127 Isaiah 46: 9-13 NIV

128 Joshua 3:5 NIV

129 Batterson, Mark. "Day 3 Amazing Things," *Draw the Circle: the 40-Day Prayer Challenge*, Zondervan. 2012.

130 2 Corinthians 6:16-17 NIV

131 Ibid.

132 Joshua 5:13-15 NIV

133 Joshua 6:2 ASV

134 "Matthew Henry's Concise Commentary," Biblehub. com, 2015.

135 Joshua 5:13-15 NIV

136 Joshua 5:15b NIV

137 Based-on-Hebrews 13:5 NIV

138 Prince, Joseph. Destined to Reign Devotional

139 Philippians 4:4 NIV

140 Colossians 1:11 NIV

141 Nehemiah 8:10 NIV

142 John 14:26, 27 NIV

143 Revelation 8:4 NIV

144 Romans 5:2-5a NIV

145 Based on Proverbs 18:21 NIV

146 Based on 2 Peter 1:3,4 NIV

147 Based on Proverbs 22:6 NKJV

148 Based on John 14:13 NKJV

149 Based on Psalm 131:1 HCSB

150 Based on Proverbs 11:23 NIV

151 Based on Proverbs 19:11 NIV

152 Based on Proverbs 22:4 ESV

153 Based on Proverbs 21:21 NIV

154 Based on Proverbs 23:18 NASB
155 Based on Psalm 112:1-9 NIV
156 Based on Psalm 68:28,30 NIV
157 Based on Psalm 24:4,5 NIV
158 Based on Psalm 25 NIV
159 Based on Nehemiah 8:10 NIV
160 Based on Deuteronomy 28:4 NIV
161 Based on Deuteronomy 28:12 NIV
162 Based on Isaiah 29:22-24; 40:11 NIV
163 Romans 8:35, 37-39 NIV
164 Isaiah 46:11 NIV
165 1 Kings 19:15, 16 NIV
166 Matthew 11:3 NIV
167 Matthew 11:4 NIV
168 Matthew 11:4 NIV
169 Matthew 11:3 NIV
170 Based on Psalm 145:13 NIV